Volume IV Number 2

Yale Anglers' Journal

An Undergraduate Publication

New Haven

Editor-in-Chief	Alexis Surovov
Administrative Director	Anna Swanson
Business & Art Director	Andrew Liverman

Editorial Board: Kate Block, David Haltom, Andrew Liverman, Wesley Ng, Will Starks, Hannah Stauffer, Alexis Surovov, Anna Swanson, Eric Werness

Advisor at Large & Co-Founder:	Joseph Furia
Advisor at Large & Co-Founder:	James Prosek
Advisor at Large:	Steve Hayhurst
Faculty Advisor:	Nelson Donegan

Mail: Yale Station, PO Box 204048, New Haven, CT 06520-4048
Phone: (203) 432-0268. Fax: (203) 432-0357. E-Mail: info@yaleanglersjournal.com
Fishing the Web: http://www.yaleanglersjournal.com

The *Yale Anglers' Journal* (ISBN 1-892441-06-3) is a registered non-profit undergraduate publication dedicated to an understanding of angling and the natural world, with an emphasis on estuaries, streams, rivers, lakes and oceans. This journal is published by Yale College students; Yale University is not responsible for its contents.

Guidelines for Submissions: Prose, poetry, art, and letters to the editors should be sent on computer disk or via e-mail in cut-and-paste text form, or, if this is not possible, by mail. **Please include a short biographical sketch.** The Journal will respond within 60 days, but will not comment or offer suggestions. Honoraria are currently not available. Submissions not accepted for a current issue may be included in a later one. Submissions will be returned upon request. Views and opinions expressed in articles in the Journal do not necessarily reflect the views and opinions of the editorial staff.

For Subscription: The Yale Anglers' Journal is published semiannually. Single copies $12, available by mail, www.yaleanglersjournal.com, or at selected bookstores. One year subscription $20; two year subscription $30. Gift cards with personalized messages can be included when subscribing a friend. Donations to the *Journal* are accepted in the form of checks made payable to Anglers' Journal.

Printed by Reprographics and Imaging Services, Yale University

Roster of Patrons

Art Editor's Note

In his *Pilgrimage to Haig-Brown*, Skip Morris describes the proper technique for fishing a pool "I tossed my little wet fly out into the main river and let it swing down into the sheltered and seemingly bottomless eddy below the island. I kept putting the fly further and further and letting it swing downstream until I felt a tug..." I attempted a similar method on our staff's most recent trip to a small river outside New Haven, and while unfortunately a decided lack of entomologically correct flies and a few ill placed bushes conspired to thwart any potential success that day, the spreading casts were strikingly reminiscent our recent efforts with the *Journal*. This year in particular we have cast word of the *Yale Anglers' Journal* across the world and have felt the tug of success with almost every extended line.

Because of the generous support of our benefactors and patrons, we were able to hold the *Journal's* first submission contest. The call for works went out to universities and individuals across the country and our post office and electronic mailboxes filled with responses. Students, professors and creative anglers submitted their literary and artistic work for review. The staff spent a number of enjoyable nights passing around slides, printouts, and scrawled handwritten works with each editor rooting for their own favorites. The artwork of Borski, the memoir by Rutter and the poems of Welti, Hardy, and Sipe were just a few of the pieces that we were able to publish in Volume 4, Number 2. Plans for another contest are already in the works and we hope word of the contest reaches even further afield and astream.

Your recommendations, as our devoted readers, have brought us many new subscribers and we urge you to keep telling friends and fellow anglers about us. We have also been working to publicize the existence of our *Journal* through other media. The launch of www.yaleanglersjournal.com into the electronic world has given us exposure to a broader audience and an accessible forum to display the *Journal*. We receive a number of emails from past readers who were excited to rediscover us after a few years and, after assuring them that we had not long since folded and that the *Journal* has a bright future, were eager to get a hold of any missed issues. Still others finding our publication for the first time proceeded to order a subscription, as well full set of back issues. A number were intrigued and impressed enough by what they saw on the website to subscribe to the upcoming issues and we hope that they approve.

In line with our expanding efforts, the art and writing of our latest volume represents a diverse catch. Thadeus Norris's humorous descriptions of fishing in a wild pre-industrial New Hampshire with all its horse drawn wagon riding and salted pork eating, represents the best in classic sporting literature. The tale along with the cartoon of Honore Daumier, assures us that the difficulties of fishing are as humorous today as they were over a hundred years ago. Ernest Schwiebert, in his fishing talk, continues to remind us that angling is hardly a purely modern pursuit and man has a long history of line fishing. However, angling remains a pertinent topic for young writers as well. The aquatic pursuit not only causes self reflection but stimulates thinking about some of the most current of social and environmental questions as seen in Michael Rudder's *Considering the High-Mountain Grayling* and Daniel Smith's piece on Aldo Leopold. Both writings ponder in their own unique ways our continued relationship to the natural world. These works and many others, equally striking in their subject and skill, speak to the thoughtfulness and talent which anglers bring to describing their pastime. Enjoy this *Journal*, and keep helping us in casting word of the *Yale Anglers' Journal* to new pools and anglers.

Tight Lines,

Andrew Liverman
Art Editor &
Marketing Director

Yale Anglers' Journal

Volume Four   Number Two

Carl Armin Hansen
The Salmon Fisher
1922

Considering the
High-Mountain Grayling:
Casting Into God's Country
Michael Rutter

IT was June in God's country-sometimes called the Wind River Mountains.

A light afternoon breeze off Elk Heart Pass rippled the icy navy-green water. The sky was a kingfisher-blue. I cast a tattered March Brown over a rocky shelf and let it bob in the film. I sensed the splash a quarter second before I saw it. I felt the pickup, hesitating slightly before lifting my faithful Sage rod to set the hook. The silver bullet went airborne, shaking his head violently, stripping away yards of line. At the least, he strained my 8X tippet.

After several desperate runs, including one dive, he mostly gave up, so I nursed the weary fighter to the spruce-lined shore. His defeated lavender dorsal fin broke the water with the quiet dignity only a grayling can muster—a respectable fish, well over a pound. I gladly set him free to eat more bugs on the rocky reefs. Maybe he'd take my fly again on another day. As he nosed into the deep water, his shiny luster dulled like a tarnished suit of chain mail and he was gone.

This warrior was many ounces shy of the Wyoming state grayling record of 2.4 pounds: Breaking the record was my solemnly-sworn life-long quest, my casting holy grail. Mind you, my yearly pilgrimage to the Winds is more than an attempt to break a foolish record or placate my vanity. I'd likely weight the monster and cut him loose, send him back to the cold waters he knows as home with my blessings. My knowing I'd caught him would be enough. Any serious caster would require no more.

My trip is really a sounding for spiritual refreshment, for life. It's more than catching exotic fish, too, since grayling aren't all that formidable to hook. Rather, it's my Affaire de Coeur, my consummation devoutly to be wished, my annual rendezvous with a courtly paramour, a fellow actor in this alpine morality play.

I love all things grayling, certainly, but mostly I love grayling colors: The splendid hues of understated lilac and icy green on the spiny sailboat dorsal fin; the fluorescent, sapphire-like periods along the body; the dusky yellow-green tail; the alluring white lips. There's much to admire. And for a die-hard fly guy, like myself, there's also what I call grayling passion, the assertive, single-minded manner in which this fish approaches life ... especially feeding. Normal adjectives mortal casters use don't seem to fit since trout and bass dining habits seem almost genteel by comparison.

A grayling never takes, picks up, or sips a dry fly. He assails it with the zeal of a Don Quixote challenging a windmill, making the feeding frenzy of a half-starved mako shark look anemic by comparison. Plainly told, a grayling must charge, like a dignified royal warrior, into what it's going to eat—then devour its food without ceremony like a teenager eating Quarter Pounders at MacDonald's. Some casters erroneously suggest a grayling is a bit equivocal about the strike. They are wrong. There's nothing equivocal about this fish, especially its feeding habits. Perhaps a reason for this misconception is the grayling, like its far removed mako shark cousin, has a tendency to do a half roll when it takes its prey. Casters, especially if they've fished chalk creeks, try setting the hook too soon, ripping the damn thing out of its mouth before the grayling has a hold. With grayling you have to pause a second, then lift up and set the fly.

You can't rush art.

A grayling's feeding directness brings tears of appreciation to even the most heartless dry-fly man. It's a fly caster's dream since a grayling taking a dry usually leaps out of the water—nailing the pattern coming down. It's a joy. And since grayling usually travel in schools, when you catch one you'll catch many. Fishing a grayling on a fly makes you proud you've never ... not even once ... disgraced a hook with a slimy wad of PowerBait.

A grayling's full-bore feeding charge is a result of its far sightedness. It has a wonderfully-tuned eye that can hone in on a struggling pinhead-sized nymph at fifteen feet. It makes a full-purpose-of-heart rush, but life is out of focus as it closes in, often missing its target by inches. An experienced caster won't despair because a grayling is a curious sort and will come back again ... and again, if you leave the fly in the water.

Isaak Walton, a patron saint, if fly casting is your religion, noticed this peculiar trait in his angling bible. He suggested, "A grayling is simpler than a trout; for he will rise twenty times at a fly-if you miss him-and yet rise again." A draper-tailor by day, Brother Isaak spent a lot of time on the water. He knew his grayling—that much is quite obvious. However, he did make one little observation that wasn't quite accurate—a misconception this fish has had to live down since the British Renaissance. Fisherman Isaac suggested grayling had a "tender mouth [and] that he is oftener lost after [being] hooked."

Even fishing saints can be a few degrees off now and then. I harbor no ill against Brother Isaak. Grayling have a small mouth, true, but it isn't any more tender than a trout's. Because of the fish's tendency to roll when striking, it's become a victim of its own far sightedness. Misses are likely, especially if you lift the rod too fast.

A stream grayling's attack is usually opposite of a trout's. A feeding trout will pick up a fly while the fly is ahead or right above its lie. Grayling, on the other hand, will usually wait for the fly to pass before going after it. This can be rather troubling to the die-hard trout boy trying his hand at hooking grayling for the first time. He's lifting his line too soon. It means a fish sees the fly, lets it drift past, then turns about to make an attack. This is something to remember if you are fishing a stream or river. Also keep in mind a grayling might trail after a fly before it initiates a slamming blitzkrieg. Unlike trout, which will frequently suspend in the water while feeding, a grayling tends to hug the bottom (this probably has something to do with it being far sighted).

Grayling aren't people shy—*you can wade in close without fouling your fishing water.* If you've fished spring creeks, or if you follow the cult dedicated to luring wily German browns to rise, you know you have to keep out of sight at all times. Such fish are inordinately spooky. More than once I've slithered up to a pool to cast my offering at a wary brown, and worn holes in the knees of my waders being sneaky .

However, if grayling aren't people shy, by trout standards, *they are very, very line shy.* Much more line shy than chalk creek trout.

If there's any fishing pressure on the stream at all, you'll need to go to extra lengths (no pun intended). Use a longer leader and cast so your fly line never drifts over the fish—which can shut grayling down in that stretch of water in a hurry. It might be a good idea to go to a 12 leader if you're in shallow water.

Every year in early June, my Trooper tugs my trailer over the mountains to a quiet lake outside Pinedale, Wyoming-my annual pilgrimage for the sacred Thymallus. It's the first official ritual that signals my summer has begun. I'm not sure if it's a crusade for grayling because it's a fish wholly pure, or for the world the fish lives in (which is also wholly pure).

While the grayling is rightly known as gullible and somewhat easy-to-catch, it's not stupid. Rather, it's a fish that's innocent in a world that is not. It has never evolved the caginess or suspect of the brown, the guile of a walleye, the determination of a steelhead, the black heart of the pike, or the tenacity of the rainbow.

I've grown to love a fish that has endured for eons, let alone a fish that survived evolution of man without distrusting the world from which it has spawned. Traces of doubt never seem to enter its mind. While an aggressive feeder, the grayling is as guileless as Billy Budd (and possibly as fated in the twenty-first century because of its naivete). The grayling doesn't know that there is evil in its universe until it's too late, and even then one wonders if its innate gullibility is ever challenged.

If something has the appearance of food, it must be food. Artificiality or falseness is never considered. Thus, the fish will charge at anything that looks edible.

As you'd expect, this fish can only live in the purest, gin-clear water. It will not tolerate more than a trace of pollution. Grayling is a meter, an environmental yardstick, if you will, we ought to monitor more closely. How the grayling survives may be indicative of our own survival, giving us clues about how we are treating the world that supports us. The grayling may be a better earth watch than all the trendy environmental ivory-tower watch groups and Washington Congressional Committees rolled in one.

In the last century around the end of the Civil War, grayling were thick in most of Michigan's watersheds. The fish was handy and plentiful; fishermen came from all around to try their favorite fly. (I suppose it was a good way to try and forget the bloodbath we call the Civil War.) Michigan grayling were written up in all the fashionable 19th century sporting journals. However, in a ten-year period, it all but vanished. The country needed wood, and Michigan logs were some of the best. The seemingly endless woods were cut with little thought for tomorrow (folks could always move west).

As a result of savage logging practices, the purity of the watershed was altered, greatly affecting grayling. Surprisingly, it did little to affect the more resilient native trout populations. At the same time, there was a commercial demand for grayling flesh, which is very tasty , in growing municipalities like Chicago and Detroit. By the late 1870s, the celebrated grayling joined the wolf, the buffalo, the passenger pigeon. It was all but wiped out in the north woods.

Grayling fishing is *at-one-ness* for the fly caster who can't separate his or her sport from theology. It's a type of atonement for having to make a living instead of throwing fly line. Casting for *Thaymallus* reminds you of what the world was like before things started creeping up on other things—before swords, before guns, before splitting atoms. Before deceptions of any kind, even cleverly tied patterns. The grayling has an Eden-like innocence about it that is refreshing in the midst of civilized madness. It takes you back to one simple truth: About the greatest thing we can do is catch fish with grace and style.

Grayling are small, but dignified. They love purity and can tolerate nothing less—still, they're fighters and a tough little fish. When you hook one, for a minute or two you'll think you've roped a Texas longhorn. If you use a light rod and delicate tippet, it's quite sporting. A grayling fights for all it's worth. It doesn't save its strength like a trout—which will let you bring it in a ways, then pour on the steam (a trout gets worn down by degrees). Grayling give all. Their first or second runs are their best. After they realize the battle is over, they give up and let you pull them in ... exhausted yes, but haughty and dignified nevertheless.

Maybe this pragmatism comes from the world they live in. It's unblemished, you can be sure, but it's often mighty cold. In many grayling waters, ice is a major factor a good part of the year. Open water in a lot of grayling country, especially as you go further north, is a luxury to be enjoyed a few months a year. As you'd suppose, this type of water might be somewhat oxygen depleted. Trout don't thrive in these conditions, but the grayling adapts nicely. They fill the niche amicably.

About the only common denominator in many grayling streams is to look for breaks in the flow—a log, a boulder, a submerged rock, a gravel bar. Grayling tend to stack in back of such obstructions since it breaks the flow and is a good place to start. If you watch the water carefully, you'll see fish moving about. It may take a little scouting, but before too long you'll locate the type of water that holds fish. Polarized glasses are a must when grayling hunting.

Rediscover your innocence.

Michael Rutter lives in the heart of the Rocky Mountains within minutes of a blue-ribbon trout stream. He fishes 100 days a year—especially if it gets in the way of work. Michael Rutter is also a Christa McAuliffe Fellow and teaches English at Brigham Young University. Michael has written forty books and numerous articles. Among other outdoor publications, he has written Fly Fishing for the Compleat Idiot *and the award winning* Fly Fishing Made Easy. Basic Essentials: Fly Fishing *will be released this summer. His articles have appeared in* Outdoor Life, Sports Afield, *and fly casting magazines.*

Henry Wolf
Fishing With Grand'pa
Print
19th Century

Running

Catherine Hardy

I've set myself
like a wheel in a rot,
feet square
on the cinders
and hear
the others panting
as they pass
or
they hear me
as I pass.
Sweat beads
collect
above my upper lip
and
my legs enjoy
their amnesia
but
after 25 laps, I hit
the wall, gag
on my own
breath, hear
the avalanche roar
of blood pumping through
as I suck in
air
for my lung's

shallow sacks
and think of
so many fish
my grandfather caught,
how they
glistened under
the naked bulb
over
his workbench
and the sound
of his knife
through their necks
and the click, click,
click, as he began
scaling.

*Catherine Hardy teaches writing and literature at the Art Academy of
Cincinnati. She is the founding editor and literary editor of* Indiner, *the Art
Academy's magazine of literature and art. She has always been a psychologi-
cal fisherwoman.*

Life's Darkest Moment

H. T. Webster
Cartoon as appeared in *To Hell with Fishing*
1932

Trout-Fishing in Northern New Hampshire

Thaddeus Norris,
Edited by William Ross

I had often heard of people catching Trout "as fast as they could haul 'em out" I had often been assured of the plausibility of such a fact, but I had my doubts. I knew I had fished for Trout, and never "hauled 'em out" at all, and so I was a skeptic as to any such proceedings as enthusiastic anglers from the north of the Granite State had repeatedly affirmed to have been within their daily experience. Taking all things into consideration, therefore, I determined to try for myself.

There were three of us: our baggage as follows: Item, one bottle of gin, two shirts—Item, one bottle schnapps, two pair stockings: Item, one bottle Schiedam , one pair fishing-pants: Item, one bottle genuine aromatic, by Udolpho Wolfe, name on the wrapper, without which the article is fictitious, one pair extra boots: Item, one bottle extract of juniper-berry; one bottle brandy, long and wide, prescribed by scientific skill for medicinal purposes. Also, rods, flies, tackle in abundance, and a supply of gin; in addition, each of us had a quart-flask in our pockets, containing gin. We also had some gin inside when we started.

Thus prepared, we started by rail from where the gin was purchased, for Littleton, which we reached in the afternoon.

Littleton is a large and flourishing community, composed chiefly of ephemeral stage drivers, black-legs, and acute landlords, who play poker with unsuspecting travellers over night, to whom they lend money in the morning to pay their tavern-bills. We did not abide in Littleton. We procured a wagon and two horses, or rather, about one and a half, and set forth about three p.m. As soon as we reached the highway, and were clear of the surrounding houses, I obtained my first view of New Hampshire scenery.

Back of us lay the lofty summits of the White Mountains—Washington, La Fayette, and Adams, towering above the rest, as those illustrious names among mankind. At the distance of twenty or thirty miles, their well--defined outlines rose against the sky in solemn, gloomy grandeur, and their immense presence seemed to annihilate the space that intervened.

I have been in the habit of thinking that my own native West is the most beautiful country upon God's earth, and, indeed, in richness of foliage and verdure, in brilliancy of color, I know of none that surpasses it. In the spring-time of the year, when everything is bursting forth in vigorous life; when the trees bud in fearless defiance of frost, and flowers bloom in bright profusion; when the corn transcends all limits of respectable growth, and the grain starts its tender shoots before the snow has quite gone, and in later summer, when the golden harvest is ripe for the sickle, and, swayed by the gentle wind, the vast field rolls like the billows of the sea; with the cultivated garden, the farm with its barns of plenty, and its presses bursting with new wine; the plain with its velvet grass, the hillside with its luxuriant vine, Nature presents no lovelier sight than meets the eye and gladdens the heart of the dweller in the Buckeye State.

Still, such scenery conveys no impression of the vast or grand, for the horizon is limited in its view. But among the mountains of the Eastern States, the landscape stretches away before you for miles upon miles, with lakes, streams and rivers, villages and farms, spread out in one great picture.

But however beautiful the sight, the sun began to get hot, and ideas of sentiment rapidly vanished, and soon arriving at one of those cool springs that burst forth from the hill-side at every few rods, we stopped to refresh our parched constitutions.

The second day's ride brought us to Colebrook , where the reign of pork begins. And here let me say a word of this staple commodity of the "rural districts."

After you get up into this country, you see nothing but pork. Not fresh pork (shades of Elia, defend us!) but salt pork, that has been pickled, brined, and put away in a barrel. They chiefly fry it, when it resolves itself into a compound of liquid grease, and a tough substance, resembling underdone sole-leather, nutritive but not attractive. They fry pork for breakfast, they do the same for dinner, and are not original in the point of supper. They fry it with their potatoes; sometimes they fry it in a skillet: I believe they use it in their tea. For two mortal weeks we had nothing but pork, until we got among the Trout, and then we had trout and pork, and pork and trout, and trout with or without pork, and pork with or without trout, according to the taste and fancy of the person porking or trouting, either or both respectively.

At Colebrook, as I said, we began on pork. It was the first I had experienced, and I thought it considerably great. Subsequent events, however, succeeded in eradicating that notion from my bosom.

Leaving Colebrook, we started for the Dixville Notch. We inquired the state of the route before starting, and were informed that, "in some places, it wasn't so good as others," which was about the extent of the information to be obtained. The people of New Hampshire are remarkably cautious in their statements and not at all prone to exaggeration, and when we learned that our route was "in some places a little rough," we thought to have a comparatively easy time of it. But, shades and ministers of grace defend us! people surrounded by the comforts of civilized life can have no idea of what roads are, or rather what a road can be, if it only has a mind to. In the first place, it is like going up and down the side of a house. In going down a steep pitch, a bottle was jolted out of the rear of the wagon, and fell over the horses' heads. That's a fact! I have the affidavits. In addition, the way is impeded by immense granite boulders, a number of feet one way, and as many the other, which seem to have been shaken out of a bag, with the profusion of a pepper-box. Then, again, there is no road to speak of at all, it having been abandoned, as we afterward learned, some ten years past; the rain also has washed out deep gulleys, where your wheels are on each side, and your horses down below, underneath the wagon. But the crowning feature is the bridges. Bridges here are made to let people through into the water; for that purpose they have large holes in them, loosely covered with brush-wood, and when the unwary traveller steps upon it, he is seen no more; and when they can't get holes big enough, they have immense logs rotted to the proper point, and when you step upon them the log caves; as it were, and you then perceive the exact purpose for which the structure was intended, as above stated. We came to one of these bridges, and two of us, having some idea relative to personal safety, declined crossing in the wagon, and got out to see it go down, and sure enough, when the near horse got in the middle, away went the whole concern, and the animal went through into the bottom of the creek.

It was not, however, so deep but that, by a judicious use of his fore-legs, he could crawl out of the hole through which he had gone down, and he came up on terra firma a wet, and, to some extent, an agitated quadruped.

This may not perhaps be interesting to the uninitiated, but one who has not witnessed cannot conceive how funny it looks, to be driving a pair of horses, and suddenly see one disappear to the extent of about one-half, his fore-legs pawing in the air, and his hind-legs somewhere else, not immediately visible, the general effect being that of an attempt to climb a tree, without any particular prospect of success. No accident, however, happened, and no other inconvenience than that of one or more legs going through every bridge we crossed.

The next day we reached the falls of the Androscoggin, but had not yet attained the trouting region. We took a boat and guide, loaded in our traps, and put out for the Megalloway. This river is crooked beyond any power of description; it is a practical exemplification of the ways of the Evil One. One minute the sun is behind you; the next, ahead; then right and left, cross the middle, up and down in every imaginable position. You have to row three miles to get anywhere, if it isn't more than twenty rods off. We reached the lower landing, at the farm where we stopped, and it was about an eighth of a mile by land, and two miles and a half by the river, to the house. Water is not a speedy means of locomotion in Northern New Hampshire.

Our first day's fishing was in the Diamond River , and a good time we had of it. I tried to keep my feet dry till I tumbled in, and then I stayed in. The water here is rapid, and the stream full of rocks, on which you step, and in you go: this is invariable.

In fishing for Trout, two things are to be observed; first, you must fall down in the water, and secondly, break your rod: N___ had broken his before he started, and soon in he went, up to his neck. To tumble down in a stream like the Diamond, beside being inconvenient, is confusing; the water carries you off your feet, and bumps you against the rocks; its roar deafens you, and you think you're going to drown; your fishing-basket goes one way, and your tackle another, and you regain your feet with a general sense of damp, to hear your friend laughing at you.

In this day's fishing we caught about seventy-five pounds of Trout among four of us. At night we returned, quite well tired, to the farmhouse which was our temporary abode. We had fried pork for supper. I believe I stated that they had pork in this country. We then went to bed, or rather to mosquitoes.

There were four of us, with two beds, in a room, which, so far from David Copperfield's being able to swing a cat in it, he couldn't have performed that feat with a kitten.

Having prepared ourselves for repose, out went the candle. and in came the mosquitoes. N___ had brought with him a concoction prepared by some medical friend, which was to keep off these invidious insects. It smelt strongly of spearmint and unclean oil. It worked, however, like a miracle, for the mosquitoes would light on our faces, and their feet would stick fast in the stuff—it had an extract of tar in it for that purpose—and by the time a small troop were thus entrapped, then you had music. Anon you would hear H___ give a rousing clap, and with an expletive state "There! I missed him!" So we rolled and tossed, till finally N___ burst out laughing, wanting to know if I was awake.

Sleep being impossible, we lit our pipes, and sat up in bed to take a smoke. Jokes were cracked, stories were told, and we made night, up in that room, comparatively hideous. Next morning we learned that there was a sick baby down stairs, and the supposition in the family was, that our noise hadn't helped its colic any.

That house will not soon fade from our memory. We slept in an attic, where the roof slanted down over the heads of the beds, so that it was not ten inches above the pillow; the roof was innocent of lath, plaster, or any of those little amenities that tend to make existence endurable. Rustic ingenuity, upon the rafters over-head, had pinned, in the character of wallpaper, certain emanations of the press, among which were the Christian Herald, Boston Post, and New Hampshire Patriot.

The strong point of this contrivance was, that all manner of bugs, spiders, and other creeping things, seemed to assemble in convention in the silent watches of the night, and essayed the climbing of these papers, which being rather much inclined, rendered the task of the insects difficult; but perseverance seemed to be a predominant trait, for all night long we heard these reptiles scratching, scraping, and rustling up and down the paper, at the agreeable distance of about a foot from our heads. Occasionally a spider, more adventurous than the rest, would drop down by his web, and alight on our faces, but he generally beat a precipitate retreat. Then, too, there was a death-watch near the headboard, and be kept up his dismal ticking as long as we were conscious. This death-watch is an abominable nuisance. Its regular, monotonous, unceasing beat, heard in fearful proximity about eleven o'clock at night, when everybody else is asleep, is enough to drive a nervous man crazy. I would rather have six-pounders fired off at me all night.

However, morning at last came, and we consulted as to what course should be taken, whether to turn homeward and fish on our way back, or strike further north. We finally concluded to adopt the latter course. We procured a guide, got a wagon, left most of our luggage, took a change of raiment, all the gin, and started. We rode about six miles to a house, which is the last one upon the extremities of civilization. From this place we were to walk over a "carry," stated to be about a mile and a half long, but which was nearer six. So we packed our traps on our backs. Our guide carried all the camp equipage. N___ had a fishing basket with the gin in it; the carpet-bag with our vestments, an axe, a rifle, a skillet, a bag of salt, a chunk of pork—they have pork in this country—some wet matches, and an overcoat: the rest of us followed with such articles as remained, piled on in a promiscuous manner.

This was my first experience in "carrying," the generic word for this sort of business, and I must be allowed to state that, as a general proposition, I do not admire this species of locomotion either in point of speed or comfort. The day was hot, and such a road! eye hath not seen, ear hath not heard, neither hath it entered into the heart of any man to conceive. It was up hill and down; through bogs and swamps; over fallen trees: encountering impenetrable thickets. A wagon-path had formerly been cut through the woods, as though some one had entertained the idea that such a route might be travelled by beasts of burden, in connection with some kind of vehicle; if such a notion was ever conceived, we can only be amused at the simplicity of the individual. The path was infested with immense rocks that were smooth and slippery with moss, and when you put your foot on them, down you went, and when you were down, the mosquitoes had you for though when in motion their attacks were suspended, yet, if you stopped, they came at you with renewed vehemence.

Slipping and falling, when you are fresh and light, is not of much consequence; but when you are tired out, and have an hundred pounds on your back, it's a fearful joke. I had trudged on till, through fatigue, I had become just desperate, and would not have made any exertion to save life itself. I stepped on the point of a stone, it was treacherous. and myself, pack and all, reposed softly in the morass. The mud was knee-deep; exhausted nature had spent all her energies; I could not move hand nor foot; the mosquitoes assailed me in legions: through an opening in the trees the sun poured down his relentless rays; I thought my hour had come, and, memory unconsciously reverting to the days of childhood. I was about beginning, "Now I lay me down,"—when I heard N___ on ahead exclaiming, at the top of his voice, in all the conscious-ness of immense and impregnable strength—"There is a plea-sure in the pathless wood."

It would have afforded me satisfaction there and then, to have knocked his head off.

We accomplished the end, nevertheless, and reached the bank of the Megalloway just above the falls, to avoid which we had passed the "carry." We found here a little flat-bottomed boat, about fourteen feet long, and amply sufficient to carry a pound of butter and a dozen eggs, and when the guide told us that we were all to go in that cockle-shell, I proceeded to narrate to him a legend relating to three individuals of age and experi-ence, who are reported to have dwelt in the State of New York, and who set forth upon a certain journey by water, in a class of sailing-craft not popularly in vogue among mariners, and with regard to whom it is confidently asserted that if their means of conveyance had been of a more permanent character, their tra-ditionary reminiscences would have been prolonged.

Our guide, however, assured us that the week before the same frail bark had brought down four men with a moose they had killed; and somewhat reassured, but still with fear and trembling, we loaded our luggage. The vessel sank in the water to within three inches of her gunwale, and we had to keep the trim so nicely adjusted that if you winked one eye without the other, you were in imminent danger of upsetting.

Once fairly started, thoughts of danger vanished, and our little boat glanced over the water at a refreshing rate.

The river was perfectly still, with no current, and its smooth surface only broken by the leap of the Trout, and the splashing start of the frightened wild-duck. High mountains arose on either side, and the river-banks were lined with scrub-by pine and birch, whose interlaced boughs rendered passage impervious except to the denizens of the forest.

Our point of destination was a place called Beaver Brook, some two miles up the stream, where it was supposed that Trout would be found. We reached there about five o'clock in the afternoon, and the sport then began in earnest. In my time I have fished, as it may be, considerable. I have fished for various specimens of the finny tribe; I have essayed Cod in

Boston Harbor, and Herring and Mackerel on the sea-coast; I have whipped almost every stream for Trout in Massachusetts and Connecticut; I have taken Salmon in the Ohio, Trout in Mackinaw and Minnesota, Perch in the Mississippi, and bobbed for Whale on the coasts of Florida, but I had not reached the acme of fishing. As before stated, I had heard all sort of "fish stories" from persons who had explored the northern regions. I had listened to their statements with silent acquiescence, but inwardly distrusting; but when the reality came, there was no exaggeration that could at all come up to the simple fact. Innocent stranger! Thou who readest these lines! Perhaps you never caught a Trout. If so, thou knowest not for what life was originally intended. Thou art a vain, insignificant mortal! Pursuing shadows! Ambition lures thee, Fame dazzles, Wealth leads thee on, panting! Thou art chasing spectres, goblins that satisfy not. If thou hast not caught a Trout, this world is to thee, as yet, a blank, existence is a dream! Go and weep. Come with me, and thou shalt see or what man was made. Thou shalt learn for what those faculties were given, that thou art wasting on minor objects. The brook rolls brightly before thee; the forest is deep and wild, and its branches hang over the stream; it leaps on with silvery laughter, like youth that bounds joyfully to the dark ocean of age. Its smooth waters dash against the rocks, and become brawling foam, as broken hopes are turned to raging passions. It darts through narrow places, over opposing obstacles, as untiring energy bursts its way through untried and devious paths. It gathers in quiet pools, and returns in gentle eddies up the stream, as the thwarted purpose, the disappointed wish recoils upon itself, or settles into sluggish apathy.

Now, put up your pole, and take your first Trout, poor innocent. Rig on your fly! Not that great big red thing—put on that little gray one with the small hook. Don't you know that a Trout is the daintiest, most delicate fish that swims? You pitch at him a bait as big as your fist, and he'll turn up his nose in disgust; but just cover the point of your hook with the smallest possible piece of worm, or take the smallest fly, and he'll go at it like a Shark. Now, do you see that dark object off yonder, lying by the side of that stone?—that's about a pound and a half: we'll have him. Pitch in your fly, and skip it over the water lively; not that way—that's down the stream; cast your fly up. If you had any sense, which you haven't, you'd know that Trout always lie with their heads up-stream and if you cast down-stream, in the first place, they'll see you, and won't bite, and if they do, you'll pull the hook right out of their mouths ; but if you throw up-stream they bite faster, and you have a better chance of striking your barb through their gills. There! Your fly touches the water; see those fellows jump at it; but those are little fellows, and don't weigh more than a quarter of a pound. Follow N___'s suggestion, and put up a notice on the bank: "Small Trout are requested not to bite!"

Now heave again. See there ! That was a pretty jump he made; but he missed. Try him once more and you'll strike, Now he's on; let your reel run: there he goes upstream. How nicely he springs out of the water! He's got frightened, and don't know what's the rumpus. Reel him in a little; don't pull too hard, or you'll break your pole; you see, it's bent double already. Just hold him tight enough to guide him, and he'll tire himself out in a few minutes; he can't stand it long, dashing about at this rate. Don't get too much excited, or he'll fool you yet. When you strike a fish you must be cool and collected. You see they are of an excitable temperament, and when they get the barb into their mouths they become agitated; they are also gamey, and make a good fight, and consequently, if you are anywise rash, and attempt to get them in too soon, ten to one you'll break your line. Now you see the rascal has started down-stream for the river, and thinks if he gets into deep water he'll be out of the way. Let him slide; let your reel go out its full length. Now he's still; he don't feel you pull, and thinks he's safe. Begin and reel him up. Now he's waked up again worse than ever, Don't he go pretty? Just hold him steady up the stream, and as his mouth is wide open, he'll drown soon ; because, if you drown a Trout be thereby becomes dead, and when dead, is in a perfectly passive state. See, his struggles are becoming feebler and feebler; you'll have him soon. Be patient: now he's still; put him up to the side of the boat, and take hold of him just behind the gills. There, isn't he a beauty? Don't those bright spots and silver stripes go to your heart? Don't you wish you were as good-looking as a Trout? Wouldn't you captivate your friends?

The shades of eve begin to fall. I sit in the foot; N___ a little below; H___ above. It is still as night, except the repeated splash of fish as they rise at the fly, or as they struggle in vain attempts to escape..

I have at various times, in various places, made various statements with regard to our success upon that particular afternoon, none of which have as yet been believed. Friends, of whom I had a right to expect better things, have upon occasions winked knowingly when I have narrated my experience; some have laughed outright; some have remarked unreservedly that that was a "fish story." Others have detected seeming inconsistencies, and irreverently asked for explanations; and again it has been inquired which was the trout, and which was the gin. I therefore will content myself with the following statement, made upon honor, that in a very short time we caught a very large number of fish.

While we were fishing, our guide was pitching our tent. Our guide was a great institution; he was a complete backwoodsman. With an axe he could do or make anything in the world. I believe he could make a watch with that axe. He could chop down a tree in no time, and in the tree he'd find a coon, or a nest of squirrels, and a whole hive full of wild honey; whereupon he'd have food and raiment for a month. He had great skill and mechanical ingenuity; and though of slight frame, his strength was enormous, and his endurance eternal. He could row a boat all day without stopping. He could climb over rocks and mountains for a week with a pack on his back, that I couldn't lift with a pair of horses. He'd be in the water for twelve hours without inconvenience. He was modest, good-natured, always ready to do anything, and was amazingly tickled to hear us talk and joke. He confined himself principally to gin. In the few days he was with us, he became very fond of us and when we parted, he rigged a sail out of my shawl, with which we rowed comfortably against a headwind for seven miles.

He was fond of woods sport. When we had finished fishing and it grew dark, we went ashore to where he had rigged our tent. He had cut a quantity of small hemlock boughs, with which he covered the floor of the tent about six inches deep, over which he spread his camp blankets, and made a couch softer than downy pillows are. He had also a huge log fire, and we made preparations to cook supper. Imprimis, a skillet is indispensable in the woods. It is convertible to many uses and purposes: you can bail a boat with it splendidly; wash your face with it; boil water and make tea, and wash the dishes; bake bread; fry potatoes, pork, and Trout, and feed the dogs with it after supper.

So we got out the skillet, cleaned a lot of Trout, cut the slices of pork (we had brought a piece of pork, and a bag containing bread and dough-nuts; to be sure, they had been in the bottom of the boat, and all got soaked, but that made no difference), and the pork hissed, and we turned the Trout with a wooden spoon and put salt on them, and then the Trout hissed; once in a while one would drop into the fire, and if the dog wasn't watching, and you were quick, you could get it again. But I had a big fight over one great fellow that tumbled out of the pan: I got him by the head and the dog got him by the tail, and it was nip and tuck, pull Dick pull devil: the dog a little ahead, for the fish broke in two, and he got mor'n half; but he subsequently choked on the back-bone, at which I was rejoiced. We rang the bell for tea. The guide made some torches of birch-bark, and stuck them up around, and we had an illuminated banquet-hall.

We spread our viands on another piece of birch-bark; each fellow took a forked stick, and then and there we fed. We then cleared away the table and washed the dishes, by throwing the birch-bark into the fire and leaving the skillet to the dog.

We then held a council of war, and concluded to cross-examine a bottle of gin. Gin has its uses in the woods. But we were without water, and had nothing but those leathern drinking-cups, holding about a gill. Here was a difficulty at once, for to be under the necessity of going down to the stream every time you wanted a drink, was not to be thought of; beside, we might be thirsty in the night. But our guide solved the problem. He took that immortal axe and went off into the woods, and came back in a minute with some large sheets of birch-bark—birch-bark is also a wonderful invention so be sit down to make a birch-bark bucket. I don't know how it's done; N___ does, and he showed me two or three times; but for the life of me I couldn't see through it. About these things I'm thick about the head. It is somehow thus: You take a large square sheet of birch-bark and some wooden pins, you turn up one end of the bark and stick in a pin, you then turn up the side and fasten it to the end; you double the ends together and fasten them with these pins; turn it up all around, so the water won't run out, fasten it, and there's your bucket; it is a very simple contrivance, and eminently practical. He got one completed, and found a knot-hole in the bottom, but finally made one that held about three quarts; so we filled it, placed it beside the tent, and began those experiments with the gin, to which brief allusion has been made.

After eating and drinking we lit our pipes. You take pipes and tobacco in this country altogether; segars are perfectly useless. I carried the tobacco loose in one of my pockets, which was a reservoir for the whole party. One has no idea of the luxury of a pipe in the woods until it has been tried; it is vastly superior to any other known method of combusting the weed. You might smoke forty segars and not obtain the same amount of satisfaction that a solitary pipe affords. Therefore we sat in the door of the tent, and as the smoke curled gracefully away we had sundry operatic performances, in which I acted the part of Prima, and N___ of base, Donna; and the woods rang with the entrancing melody of our voices; while afar off we heard the hoot of the owl, and once in awhile the scream of a wildcat; but we were not at all alarmed. I should not omit to relate one of my troubles, and that was in the way of boots. A kind friend at Hanover lent me a fine pair of fishing-boots, that came almost up to my ears, and had great big legs to them. I first fished with them in the Diamond River. I endeavored to maneuver so as not to go over boot-top, but pretty soon I tumbled in, and when I got up my boots were full of water, and weighed about two tons apiece; so I waded ashore for the purpose of eliminating the element. I laid down on my back, and raised my heels up in the air, and the ultimate consequences were, that the whole quantity of fluid found its way out at the back of my neck, just below the left ear. During our whole trip the great occasion of the day was the getting my boots off.

Many of you know what wet boots are; I had them in perfection. Our guide was a first-rate boot-jack, otherwise I should be wearing the articles at the present day. I lay down on the floor, N___ would take hold of my shoulders, the guide and H___ hold of my boots, and we would work, and twist, and accomplish the feat, or rather feet, in about an half-hour. Item, when fishing for Trout, wear shoes.

Boots off, and otherwise happy, we lay in the tent, smoked, and employed ourselves in the charms of conversation. Our guide had gone off into the woods some distance, and soon we heard a crackling and snapping as though the world was about to conflagrate. We rushed out of the tent, and saw, off in the forest, a large tree all on fire from turret to foundation stone. It flashed, and blazed, and roared, and I thought the whole wilderness was going, so I seized a few articles of value, and was about to take to the water for safety, but was restrained by N___, who said it was some of the guide's work, which it proved to be. Birch trees are covered with a light bark, which every year peels off to about the thickness of a sheet of paper; this dies, and drying, becomes like tinder, and is used as such; and if you touch a match to the root of a tree, the blaze flashes up in a moment over every limb, and makes as fine a specimen of indigenous firework as may be desired. The night was very dark, and there the tree stood, every limb and branch, all in a blaze, and lighting up the forest like day. The wild birds started from their roosts, flying helter-skelter; deer and other vermin were scampering in promiscuous confusion, and altogether it was pleasant. Soon another tree started, and then another, and soon half a dozen, in all directions; and to us, who were novices, the spectacle was beautiful. Our guide soon came back—he had been prowling round in his stocking feet—and we all went to bed.

The next morning we all went to fishing, and fished to our hearts' content; in fact we became perfectly satiated and disgusted. They bit so fast, and we caught so many, that we lost all relish for it. We filled our boat almost full. Anything less than a half pound in weight we threw back into the water; and after we all got sick of it, we agreed to take down our poles and not put them up again in that part of the country. About eighty pounds of the largest we concluded to take home with us; so our guide made a species of box out of elm-bark, in which we salted down our fish, to pack on our backs.

I have thus given an outline of one day's occurrences, and the others were like unto it. We had just as much Trout-fishing as we wanted. We eat so many that we almost killed ourselves; and finally came to the conclusion that Trout were not what they were cracked up to be, after all.

Although a number of authors predate Thaddeus Norris in the writing of American angling books, it is he who is most often identified as "America's Izaak Walton." Norris' The American Anglers Book reflected American angling experience unlike any previously published work. Norris discussed such topics as dry fly fishing and stream conservation long before they were fashionable. At the end of his opus, he closed with a section entitled "Dies Piscatoriae," because to him, appendix sounded too much like a useless appendage. On the contrary, his local color accounts of the exploits of he and his friends, of which this is my favorite, are not only entertaining, but prove that in the hands of a good writer any truth can be sufficiently stretched.

William E. Ross is an Associate Professor and Head of the Milne Special Collections and Archives at the University of New Hampshire, Durham, NH. He holds both masters in history and library science from the University of Maryland and a Ph.D. from American University. Among the diverse collections under his supervision is the Milne Angling Collection, one of the largest and most up-to-date angling collections in the United States. He resides in Dover, New Hampshire with his wife and three children. In his ever-decreasing spare time, he ties flies and fly fishes for everything from native brook trout to striped bass. And, early every summer, he and his boys return to fish the headwaters of the Diamond River that Norris so colorfully describes in this account.

Harold Malette Dean
Day dream
Print
1939

Sea Monsters

Susan Borden

AS a child growing up in Iowa, I was fascinated by the idea of aquatic monsters. I would scan the shelves of the city library, which smelled strongly of smoke after the fire, searching for books about the Loch Ness monster, the beast of Lake Champlain, and assorted mysterious swimmers in the open ocean. Then I would pore over the eyewitness accounts ("it had a head like a horse, and a whitish mane straggled over its long neck"), the sketches, and the grainy black and white photographs, most of which showed little more than gently undulating shapes in the water. I was utterly convinced that the accounts were all true, that deep in rivers, lakes, and seas there lived a variety of sleek, agile water monsters. I imagined them paddling with diamond-shaped flippers, preying on silvery fish, darting their small, keen, heads in underwater caverns, and I was content.

"It could happen," I explained to my ever-patient mother. "There was this fish, a coelacanth, it's called, and the scientists thought it had been extinct for millions of years, but they found some alive! It's a living fossil, and the Loch Ness monster could be like that. A left-over plesiosaur! Loch Ness used to be open to the sea, and it could've stayed and lived there even after the land came up. It's a really deep lake, and there are lots of fish and the water's dark... ." My mother listened. She wanted the monster to be real too, for my sake.

I dreamed once about a water monster, one of those extra vivid dreams that you remember all your life. In reality, the yard behind our house tended to become a slough in the spring, with pools of standing water suitable for wading if I wore my mother's rubber boots. In the dream I saw the yard submerged, not just in small pools, but in a flat spreading lake. As I watched, the grey lake began to roil and the monster surfaced. I can still see it in my mind's eye—coils rising, wearing a tapestry of black scales that winked in the sunlight, turning to let the water pour off. Its head was not like a horse's; it was like a dragon's, large and furious. For one thrilling moment, the glittering eyes looked into mine, and then the monster exhaled vapor and crashed into the lake once more. I recall clearly the buoyant swell of joy I felt in the dream, knowing that a monster lived in my own backyard lake. I could watch for it and surely catch sight of it again and again. It would live in the lake and never be captured-no, never that. This is the only dream that I remember from my childhood.

About this time, my brother happened across an ancient beige and yellow fishing pole in the basement, the small hoops that guided the line now brown with rust. He used it to play with the cat. I used it to fish in the backyard slough. Wearing my mother's white rubber boots, which buttoned at the side with a figure-eight piece of elastic, like a child's rain boots, I cautiously strode through the standing water. The drowned grass swirled lightly before me, and bits of sediment blossomed in the murky water with each step I took. Carefully drawing the poleback and to the side, I released the sticky lever on the reel and let the aged fishing line fly. There was no hook at the end of it—just two split-shot weights and a faded gold clip, on which lures could be attached. I was not allowed a hook or lures, but the clip looked promising somehow. Knowing full well that there was nothing to catch in the skim of rainwater, I fished nonetheless, hopefully, misguidedly, still carrying visions of sea monsters behind my eyes.

Within weeks the pools would draw in upon themselves, grow shallow, and disappear, leaving behind fetid mud and then mats of tangled, yellowish grass, which we children had to rake up. Not so much as a tadpole survived. There had never been any tadpoles to die.

The notion of sea monsters subsided as I grew older. The early morning fishing jaunts of high school, which usually yielded only a small whiskered catfish or two, trailed off after my friends went off to college, I stayed home, unwillingly. Then a slashing blow fell. My mother died suddenly of something from which she should not have died. She was fifty-seven and I was twenty. I kept my head down, oppressed by the same streets and the hot, green fields of corn that banded the city and flowed over the countryside. I felt unable to escape from the shrinking pool of my own circumstances. Eventually, I rallied feebly enough to send away for information about study abroad programs. Gingerly, fearful of failure and disappointment, I reached out for something new.

That first trip to England for a summer school course brought me around and shook me out of my lethargy. The next summer I went to Great Britain again, eager for reassurance that the world was big, that I could travel, that I could change. England introduced me to the sea and Scotland to deep lakes, which seemed like the sea temporarily captured. The ragged, rocky shorelines under solemn skies intrigued me more than any tropical beach; these waterscapes possessed the rasp of real life. Their roughness matched my mood, and, paradoxically, made me happy. On my third trip to Great Britain, I tentatively planned a journey to Loch Ness. It had always been one of my goals in life to see it, yet I feared my first glimpse. Would it be ringed with deluxe condos? Would wrappers from Wimpy's hamburgers drift on its surface? Would I be forced to give up my long delight in sea monsters after all?

I have a photo of myself from that trip to Loch Ness, aged twenty-seven, taken by one of my traveling companions. The grey-blue loch ripples in the foreground and smoothes to pewter near the horizon. Clouds sail in a white sky , dropping shadows on the heathery hills. The grass is high and full of tussocks and small flowers that look like daisies, but aren't. I sit on a low stone wall, my head and upper body outlined against the loch. I am wearing the scarlet argyle sweater that I'd found lying on a London street several weeks before, blue jeans, leather sneakers scuffed in the grass. The wind has tousled my hair, which is still brown and golden, and I have abroad, genuine smile on my face. No silhouette of a graceful serpent's head and neck appears behind me, yet I remember how glad and lightsome I felt, being at Loch Ness after so many years of longing. This is my favorite photograph of myself I keep it on the desk where I write, hoping it will give me inspiration.

Nowadays I live in Minnesota. Is it a coincidence that I moved to the land of 10,000 lakes? During the years when I struggled through graduate school and then a series of pitiful part-time jobs, I promised myself that after I finally landed a good job and saved some money, I would buy a canoe. On the same day that I started that "good job," I had my first date with Pete, who would become my husband several years later. He had a canoe! On our second date we paddled White Bear Lake on a serene day in September, and we spent many hours and afternoons afterwards, paddling and fishing. I loved gliding over the cool translucent water, watching the tiny sunfish flash through glades of underwater plants and fire away from the prow of the canoe. The fish moved every which way, up, down, sideways, and diagonally, navigating many planes while I was stuck mostly in one. And when we reached the deeper water and Pete let the anchor rope slide between his fingers, I put down my paddle and peered into the lake. The shafts of slanting sunlight couldn't probe far here, and I felt both frustrated and intrigued that I could not see into the depths. Anything could be down there!

I had not fished since high school, so I had years of catching up to do. We fished every summer weekend, and some weekday evenings, too, talking quietly, eating sandwiches while the canoe rocked, guarding the red and white bobbers zealously. And when my bobber jigged coyly, paused, and then dove under the water's surface, I was ready with a sharp pull and the breathless phrase, "Got one." I reeled madly, the line zinging and throwing out stray sparkles, the rod arcing enticingly. The weight of a fish on the line, even a small fish, delighted me. Up through tiers of lake water I drew the fish; it jerked and swam madly to the side, but could not escape the hook and line. When I pulled it up into the air and saw it spinning on the line, its fins flipping helplessly and its gold and black eye staring, I felt a gust of guilt and wanted only to return it to the water. Wetting my hand to avoid disturbing its coating of protective slime, I gingerly grasped the cool, struggling body, and, as gently as I could, removed the hook from its pouting mouth and opened my hand at the water's surface. The fish flapped back into the lake, drilling downward and out of sight. Gone for good. Exhilarated, guilt-free, and once again eager. I strung another half-worm on the hook and flung the line out into the dusk as far as I could.

One evening, late, the bobber disappeared decisively with no preliminary dancing; it had been floating passively on the surface, and then it was gone, with seemingly no action in between. The taut line sprang straight down, as if I had hooked the lake itself. I heard Pete's excited commentary, but couldn't listen; I set my feet more firmly in the bottom of the sandy canoe and began to turn the reel's handle, fumbling at first and then finding a smoother rhythm. The weight on the line, the powerful pull emanating from the water, the slight list of the canoe in the direction of whatever swam below—these things filled me with anticipation and fear.

Then the connection snapped. The weight vanished along with the sense that I had something alive attached to my rod, and my line floated in the slight breeze. Crestfallen, I examined its shorn end. Only the bobber remained; hook, worm, and sinkers had vanished. "It was probably a northern," Pete said. "They'll bite right through the line unless you have a steel leader tied on." I sat slumped in the prow, my grey life jacket pushing up around my ears. "Here," he leaned forward with his smallest tackle box in his hand. "We have plenty more hooks and sinkers. " I flipped open the box and caught a whiff of the familiar scent of worms, metal, plastic, and lake water. And then I straightened my back, clipped off the end of the fishing line with the scissors from my Swiss Army knife, selected a hook, and tied it on.

The surface of the lake was calm, opaque, mysterious. I imagined snouts nuzzling through green fronds, flat eyes peering though layers of water, currents flowing over agile bodies, and the last light filtering down to touch rowing fins and glittering scales. Anything could be down there, I believe.

Susan Borden lives in St. Paul and fishes in nearby waters: Lake Phalen, White Bear Lake, the St. Croix River, and the Cascade River. She also travels gladly to the Boundary Waters Canoe Wilderness Area in northern Minnesota for paddling, camping, and fishing every year or so. She teaches writing courses at the University of Minnesota.

A well known landscape painter and illustrator, Jared Clackner's paintings have been included in exhibitions all over the United States and he has had several one man shows. The Christopher gallery in Cohasset Massachussets is currently showing an exhibit of his work and some of his paintings are visible there at www.christophergallery.com/currentexhibitionT.html. He can be contacted directly by phone at (973) 627-1226 or by mail at 48 Tomahawk Tr. Denville, NJ 07843.

Julius J. Lankes
The Crabber
Woodcut
1928

Deschutes River Confessional

Brently Johnson

I ask forgiveness from the cattails
crushed to get here, for the relief
felt relieving myself on sagebrush
and thistledown. I forfeit my rights

to rod and reel, the wicker creel
choked with fronds of fern
and the singing line that slurs
through air causing crawdads

to dance backwards
on their bent-spoon tails.
But just as I stand on a penitent
shore, there's a ripple on my sorrow,

then a heart's leap to the surface
of afternoon hatches of wings.
I hover in the cherubic clouds
of caddis burst from alder cover

and shuck the shell
of late August darkness, casting
out demons with a five weight wand.
Back into that buoyant

world of baptismal light and cosmic swirl,
I wet my hands before holding
the body of water itself,
then break the river like bread.

Brently Johnson is twenty-eight years old, currently enrolled in the MFA program at the University of Idaho. Previous to beginning graduate school, he was a fly-fishing guide in Bend, Oregon. This upcomming summer he is planning an independent poetry project on Idaho rivers and their ecological and spiritual significance on our lives.

Emil J Kosa Jr.
The Old Fishing Fleet
Etching
20th Century

Pilgrimage to Haig-Brown

Skip Morris

Here is the opinion that Roderick Haig-Brown forced me to adopt as my own, as he stated it in *Fisherman's Fall*:

Fishing is not a sport I expect ever to exhaust or abandon.

"Forced" may seem too strong a word, but it's not—the seductive power of *Fisherman's Fall, A River Never Sleeps,* and all his other books that plucked me from my chair and set me in his boots, the current breaking around my legs and riverbed gravel crunching beneath my feet, the power of his books that filled my head with his fascination for fish and water was too great for a boy with fishing in his blood to resist. I knew even as a teenager that I, too, would never exhaust or abandon fishing. Haig-Brown had me hooked, played out, and landed, and I admired him for it. He was, I felt, a master of words, a spell-caster who understood the thrill of the singing reel, the defeat of the broken tippet, and the wonder of peering into a trout pool better than any other writer possibly could, and conveyed them with unmatched clarity and force. The power of his prose had to come in part from his living in the finest little fishing area in the world—I was convinced of that. But how I believed this in spite of the vastness of his Canadian home province of British Columbia with its multitude of rivers and lakes and the great extent of its intricate coastline is now, to me, something of a mystery. There is a wealth of wonderful fishing throughout British Columbia, of course, but it never even occurred to me that any of it could compare with his little part of Vancouver Island.

So, once he'd got me addicted to fishing, the man's passion for his waters, and the waters that inspired such passion, set me to planning a fishing trip to the country that leapt so appealingly from the pages. Such a trip seemed reasonable to me—our home near Seattle, Washington lay fewer than three hundred miles south of Haig-Brown's farm on Vancouver Island; just a modest drive, I figured. So I began working on Dad. I wheedled. I nudged. I dropped hints to keep the issue on his mind. And all this time I was appealing to Mom, knowing she'd be the easier of the two and that if I could get her to work her own angle, he'd have little chance of holding out. It took some doing, but I wore him down, with Mom's help of course.

My soonest opportunity for such a distant trip would be Easter Break, an escape of around two weeks from the chaos and tyranny of high school. It would be early in April, a difficult time for fishermen, when streams can be high or even flooding from icy runoff or rain or both, and when fish may still be sluggish and unresponsive with blood winter-thick, creeping through drowsy dead-cold flesh. None of this concerned me, of course, or even occurred to me—I was, after all, only fifteen years old, an innocent. And anyway, how could fishing ever be less than excellent in Haig-Brown's waters?

Easter Break came at last, and early one brisk April morning my friend Don and I heaped our tackle into the trunk of Dad's big sedan, and then swung wide the doors and hopped into the back seat for the trip. I seemed hardly to depress the car seat, half-floating in the soft mist of anticipation. Don and I chatted openly about fishing and softly in private about girls as we rode the freeway up the Washington coast to the Canadian border just south of Vancouver—as we waited in the long line to get through customs, I could distinctly feel my full weight on the pillowy car seat, and the area of contact was growing uncomfortable. Still, my enthusiasm remained high. We left the border and headed for the ferry terminal. Getting through the ferry line took over an hour, though it seemed more like all day. Even the topic of girls was losing its interest. The ferry left the mainland and plodded across the ribbon of water separating it from Vancouver Island and the small city of

Nanaimo, which, on our arrival, seemed dark and industrial; it was reassuring to watch it fade behind us as the road drifted into a magical corridor of dense coastal forest. Within an hour, the promise of Haig-Brown's country had grown much smaller as the distress in my buttocks had grown much larger. What was that car seat made of anyway, stone? But on we continued up the elongated island's eastern side, through a few hamlets, and across a few streams of varied size, the sort I'd normally have strained to examine from the bridges but instead hardly turned my head to notice, and on and on through dull, repetitive, and unceasing forest on my pilgrimage to Haig-Brown. By now my buttocks ached deeply. I was bone-tired, and it showed. Don didn't look too good either. About the time it seemed we'd never reach at our destination, cheerful country yards and houses and side roads, mottled in shadow and low sunlight, began telling encouragingly of the approaching town. I let out a heavy sigh and stretched the stiff, weary muscles down my back.

Roderick Haig-Brown had no idea we were coming—in fact, no idea we even existed. I had neither written him nor told Dad of my intention to meet him. But Dad seemed happy to drive slowly along the road that flanks the south side of the river and watch for a mailbox saying "Haig-Brown." As we crept up the tree-lined side-road, my head filled with bright images from his books, three of which lay beside me on the car-seat: the magnificent Canyon Pool on the Campbell River and the schools of big sea-run cutthroat trout that once milled about it in August, until it was desecrated and murdered by the dams and their penstocks that permanently starved the pool of fresh current; the good run of little steelhead that surprised him by suddenly appearing a dozen years after the dams were installed; his bright, lazy days of three-quarter-pound trout on Buttle Lake, with the always present chance that one of its eight- or ten-pounders would venture up from the depths for his fly; his failed but joyful mission to really figure out the movements and feeding patterns of sea-run cutthroats in the estuaries. We soon found the mailbox bearing his name and standing before his home and his farm on the banks of the

Campbell River in the outskirts of the village named for the river and stretching upstream from its mouth.

He came to us in his driveway in a manner far too casual for the event—Roderick Haig-Brown standing right there was an event!—and asked could he help us. Dad explained that I was a great admirer of his work as I looked down at Dad's shoes. We each shook his hand, and he invited us in.

I cannot trust my memory of Haig-Brown, his home, or what happened there—I was young and overwhelmed by the presence of the man, and, of course, it all happened three-and-a-half decades ago. Nevertheless, this is how I remember it. His den was as elegantly somber as I'd imagined it. There were tall bookcases of dark wood displaying the dark spines of books; narrow windows peered out across a field to the river but allowed in only enough light to disperse a soft glow throughout the room. There was a small stone fireplace, too. A pair of coal-black Labrador retrievers lay in the corner, anxious but in obedient restraint. It was perfect. Well, almost perfect—the tiny table by the window and the fly-tying vise and few tools that lay upon it were a disappointment. I'd expected bins of feathers and hides, racks of floss and thread and bright tinsels, a long row of bright metal tools, certainly much more than the few tools on that insignificant little wooden square for such an important operation.

The dogs rose and came to us together with wagging tails and curious noses. Haig-Brown scolded them gruffly and they moped back to their corner. I knew he'd be stern with them—I knew the man, I felt—but I knew also that they'd have his respect.

Haig-Brown himself seemed entirely perfect, a looming but graceful man built all of long bones—long torso, long arms, long hands and fingers—speaking few but well-chosen and elegantly ordered words, reserved, and with just the right balance of gentleness and firmness. He seemed exactly the man to write of fishing with such passion.

I stood mostly in awestruck silence, but managed to ask about the fishing: Were the lakes going yet? Were the salmon fry out in the rivers and the cutthroats coming up from the salt to feed upon them? He seemed dubious about our chances of finding really good fishing anywhere now, as though, to my surprise, the odds were somehow against us, though we at least had some hope. The Campbell River, he said, would be as good as anyplace to start. He described a pool below an island he said we'd recognize, but he warned us that we'd have to cross to the island and that that would be difficult if the river was up. This sounded like just the sort of reasonable put-up-or-shut-up challenge I'd have expected from him. I remembered his telling in *A River Never Sleeps* how Major Greenhill had made him strip naked and then swim across an icy English river in January after two felled mallards because Greenhill's retriever was too old for the job. Whatever I was up against, I figured it had to be short of that.

There was nothing more to say except thank you, which we did, and then left for the place he had recommended on his river. When we got there, the island he'd described lay across a considerable side channel. The time it took to scramble into my waders and fumble the line and leader up through the guides seemed interminable. As soon as I'd tied on the fly I realized I'd missed a guide with the line, and so had to cut off the fly and repeat nearly the whole operation. I was considering taking up swearing. When finally I charged in, I felt the cold force of the river, and the surprise of it made me hesitate. Then I really looked the channel over for the first time, and it looked tough. But I was determined to make it across, to prove myself worthy of Haig-Brown's country, his rivers, and his fish. A little way out I realized that it was tough wading, felt the fear that comes with dubious control out in strong current, and vaguely recalled a line from his *Fisherman's Summer*. It goes as follows:

Wading upstream over a bottom of great round slippery rocks—and the Campbell has little else—is bad at any time...

Though I was wading across stream, not upstream as in his line, it seemed about as difficult as you could ask. I pushed on, though impressing Haig-Brown suddenly seemed a minor thing compared with remaining upright. Once out on the island, after the moment of relief had passed, I sensed something familiar. The smell of swollen water, the chill damp air, and the dark, green-tinged current sweeping threateningly by all felt like just another gloomy Washington river in spring. Still, this was Haig-Brown's familiar, gloomy river, so while holding fast to my high expectations I tossed my little wet fly out into the main river and let it swing down into the sheltered and seemingly bottomless eddy below the island. I kept putting the fly out further and further and letting it swing downstream until I felt a tug, followed by nothing. Then I felt another tug, struck, and a couple of dozen feet of line spun off the reel. The current weighed on the line and the fish fought as hard as it should have, so it was a while before I slid him up the gravel bar below the island. He was a splendid sea-run cutthroat of about fourteen inches, thick, silvery, and handsomely spotted— a perfectly suitable fish for the occasion. I killed him with blows from a rock, as I often did back then (though I wouldn't now) and dropped him into my wicker creel.

Nothing else came to the fly, so I waded back across, pretty much forgetting about Haig-Brown again for a little while. Don had stayed wisely with the near, safer shore, but had caught nothing.

It was almost dusk, so we took down our rods and packed our tackle away into the car. As I cleaned the fish in the river, I had what seemed a wonderful notion: why not give the trout to Haig-Brown? It would be a thank you for his fishing advice, I said, but I knew it was really to show the master that I was a fisherman worthy of his river and his respect. It seemed perfect.

He would come out as before, I imagined; then he'd silently marvel at the wonderful trout when I raised it from the creel. He wouldn't say it, but he'd judge me a fine fisherman. I could picture him hoisting the fish himself and nodding in approval of both it and me.

But when we pulled in, his wife, Ann, came out. She said he was gone right now. I stammered out that I'd met him earlier that day and had brought him a fish from the Campbell. "Did you take it on the fly?" she asked, beaming. I told her yes I had, right where he'd suggested I fish. "Oh, Roddy will be so pleased that you took it on the fly! I'll fix it for him tonight, while it's still fresh." She took the fish, thanked us, and we drove away.

I sat reveling in proud achievement, even though things hadn't gone quite as I'd imagined, and trying to forget I'd heard the great Roderick Haig-Brown referred to as "Roddy." I casually picked up *A River Never Sleeps*, opened it at random, and began reading contentedly. After a couple of paragraphs I came to this line:

"I do not fish for fish to eat; having to eat fish is one of the penalties of having been out fishing and with this penalty in mind I probably fish a little less often and less painstakingly than I otherwise would."

Skip Morris is the author of eight books on fly-fishing topics to date, mostly fly-tying books. These include Fly Tying Made Clear and Simple, The Art of Tying the Nymph, The Art of Tying the Bass Fly, *and* Morris & Chan on Fly Fishing Trout Lakes *among others. Skip also writes columns for* Fly Tyer *and* Fly Fishing and Tying Journal *magazines and is a frequent contributor to most of the American fly-fishing periodicals. He lives with his wife, Carol, and their four cats on Washington's lush and sparsely populated Olympic Peninsula.*

Tim Borksi
Curio Night Heron/Red Fish
Watercolor
2000

In the Last Year of Hemingway's Dreams

Dennis Sipe

They say that Hemingway in his sleep
sometimes saw a flash of light.
Then Serengeti heat
opened his pores and soaked his sheets.
Roars of initiated lions and hyena jokes
seeped into the dark cafe of his dreams
like smoke and lover's vengeant words
until M'cola scratched his tent flap,
spoke his name,
handed him a mug of leafy tea with milk.
After fried eggs, apricots, and Grant's gazelle hash,
dawn was still coming on an hour off.
Hemingway shouldered his rifle.
He rode in the hunting car with M'cola
to a good place, the tracker said,
to hunt that day.
Ernest hoped death was on no one's side,
that his eye and finger and heart could hold,
be all the luck that ever was,
all the religion he would need
to pray softly his will into a buffalo
quivering in heat waves.

Or, it might be that after the burst of light
Hemingway would again be
at the wheel of the Pilar

with the sun out of the Gulf Stream
like a flare lifted from its burning underwater.
The Lycoming engine arrogantly whipped
a froth into the green sea.
The writing would wait for a day.
While he read squint lines on Dos Possos's face
or any sign of weakness in Perkin's arms or legs.
While he worked their fighting of fish out like a dance to the
tick of a well oiled Hardy reel.
While he used and cursed the wind
and loved it for its indifference.

*Dennis Sipe was born in Seymour, Indiana. He has a B.A. in English from Indiana
University. He has lived in Alaks where he di work toward an M.F. A., and on Great
Cranberry Island off the coast of Maine where he worked in a boatyard. When he lived
in Arlington, Va. he was Community Relations Coordinator for the Pentagon Centre
Borders. A regular contributor to the Journal, he writes almost as well as he coordi-
nates. At last check, he was living outside Bloomington, Indiana with his wife and two
children.*

James Swann
Lakefront(Chicago)
Dry Point with Aquatint
20th Century

All is Not Gold

Dana S. Lamb

I was brought up on dry flies and brown trout. Before I married Edgar I had many a marvelous moment on the Mongaup; learned to float one of Art Flick's stiff-hackled black spiders ever so close to a certain rock on the Brodhead; took a twenty incher by the culvert on the Beaverkill, and learned how difficult it was to avoid an almost imperceptible but fatal drag in the Wilmington Notch.

Though I took Edgar to the Esopus and the Schoharie over long weekends and even spent a week with him fishing the Battenkill and the Mettowee, somehow he just didn't seem to be able to get the hang of it. He'd done some wet-fly fishing in Maine for land-locks and brook trout but the technique of the dry fly or of an upstream nymph completely eluded him.

However, he did have the time of his life when Dad took us for a week's salmon fishing on the Miramichi. And although I thought the business of casting endlessly over the side of a canoe for fish I couldn't see was rather dull, he took to it like a duck to water.

When the children came along I put away my tackle, but Edgar found a spot on the Matapedia where he could fish the last week in August and that's where he spent his vacations. Anyone who knew anything about salmon could have told him that that was the worst possible time to fish that river since the fish, six weeks up from salt water, were stale and gravid. I don't consider such fish good to eat but Edgar even made a practice of shipping these soft red salmon home to friends. And although I sought to discourage him he often, if he was feeling flush, sent one home to me. By complicated cookery I usually managed to make the thing edible though I assure you it was never appetizing.

Last August it was so hot in the city that I was delighted to have the opportunity of sending the children out to their grandparents on Long Island and almost wished that I had gone with Edgar to Matapedia. To make the city even more unattractive the garbage collectors chose that inopportune moment for their strike. Naturally I ate out as much as possible, and one particularly hot evening I was delighted, after the Bowers' cocktail party, to have them invite me for dinner at their roof garden overlooking the river. I got home about ten o'clock and although the air conditioning was on I realized as soon as I entered the apartment that all was not well. My nose led me to the pantry and there on the dishwasher was the unwanted salmon box, its top thoughtfully loosened by the janitor now retired for the night. Inside, in an advanced stage of decomposition, lay a great red hookbill balefully staring at the ceiling. Clearly prompt and drastic action was in order and I was strictly on my own.

On the shelf above the icebox was Edgar's old suitcase, the one his fraternity brothers had given him when we were married. It didn't look so bad from a distance but inside it was all coming to pieces and I'd been begging him for years to get rid of it. I put it down on the floor and after I'd gotten the ice out of the salmon sarcophagus I turned it over and the dead fish dropped into the suitcase with a plop. I stuffed some newspapers in on top of him as well as a bathrobe and some old clothes I wanted to throw away. Then I latched and strapped up the bag and staggered out into the hall. It was awkward and heavy as lead but I managed to get out onto the sidewalk where I hoped to hail a taxi. My plan was to drive to the Battery and bribe the driver to help me dump it into the river.

One disadvantage of living in Greenwich Village, however, is that there are few cruising taxicabs, and shady characters are some-times to be encountered in the darker streets. I had on my best bib and tucker so I felt somewhat nervous on this account and, instead of standing still and waiting for a cab to come by, I struggled as best I could toward the subway. As I neared its entrance the thing I greatly feared came upon me in the form of a tough and evil-looking giant of a man who seemed definitely out of character in offering to help me with my suitcase. Of course I refused his offer but he persisted and following me down the subway steps, as we approached the turnstile, roughly seized my burden and preceded me onto the deserted platform. The doors of a train were just at the point of closing and with a rush he leapt aboard, barring my attempt to follow.

Gone was the thief with my not so precious burden. I turned and hurried back to the apartment; I built myself a tall, cool drink and scribbled a hasty note to Edgar. "Darling, your beautiful salmon arrived today. I am so excited. It is almost a pity that it will be all gone when you get home. I hope you hooked a good one today. Devotedly, Kay." I didn't add, "I did." I thought of the modem-day Bill Sykes excitedly opening the suitcase in the secrecy of his broiling bedroom, and I smiled as I curled comfortably up in bed with a little volume by John Tainter Foote. The air in the apartment once more was cool and sweet.

Starting Out

The peepers in the pond are silent and thunder mutters in the April sky. Although the trout are not yet surface feeding and the salmon schools are far at sea, let's load the car before the rain. The starting of a fishing trip is the finest time of all, when all the joys we look for lie ahead; when nothing will go wrong and everything is possible; when hope and happiness ride with us at our side.

A fishing trip is as full of thrills as a plum pudding is of raisins. Some say the supreme moment comes when, from far off, they glimpse their favorite river. Others look forward most to arrival at the camp: the old familiar sights and sounds and smells; the hearty greetings from the dock or doorway; the smell of wood-smoke from the cabin's welcome fires; the merry ring of axe out by the woodpile; the lovely liquid little belltones of the wood thrush.

The dedicated dry-fly man may say that tops is when, having found the correct imitation of the natural fly, avoided getting hung up on the back cast and solved the problems of the perfect float, he sees the rise and sets the hook.

The salmon fisher often times will say there's nothing like the first firm heavy pull that tells him that the battle is joined, though others who journey with him to the Maritimes may cherish most the thought of breathlessly long runs or leaps that stop the angler's heart.

Some seek their satisfaction from an entry in the record book. Others love the rivers better than their fish. Perhaps they like the gently flowing quiet places where trout lie waiting for the mayfly beside the weaving water weeds, while swallows skim the satin surface of the stream. Some feel exalted by the spray and spume in gorges and by waterfalls in rough wild rivers running hell for leather to the sea.

Some love best the friendships made along the stream. No dairy maids these days perhaps, but brother anglers— nobler than the rest—who now and then confide that "There's a big one by that stone," and say, "You try for him." Or, "Don't you have a nighthawk number eight? Well here, take mine." Or, yet again, "Here, take this sandwich. I've had all I want."

Then others like it best, I think, when they come home and see again the family that they love—their captive audience; the dog who greets them with wild howls of happiness and frantic cart-wheels of delight; the luxury of proper baths, clean clothes, and lemon peel and ice; the hero worship at the party at the Country Club where the big brought-home salmon or the once-in-a-life-time trout lies grandly, surrounded by water cress from little brook trout streams near home.

But whatever priceless item from the beautiful bundle of a fishing trip especially delights one's heart, the greatest thrill of all is starting out, since therein is the entire treasure of what may be to come. And so, as now the raindrops splash the windshield of our car and lay the dust on little far-off country roads, we feel the freshness and the ecstasy of early morning in the springtime of our lovely ageless little world.

Author of Bright Salmon and Brown Trout, Not Far From the River *and* Woodsmoke and Water Cress, *Dana Lamb brought the voice of the fisherwoman to the angling community that has been at times sadly male dominated. Her writing has assured many lonely fishermen that for the right woman the smell of trout is an appropriate cologne and a picnic and the evening hatch beat a candlelight dinner and a movie as a good second date.*

Norman Wilkinson
Ghillie
From *The Ultimate Fishing Book*
1925

Boyhood Remembered

Russel H. Goddard

AS a little boy and until I was in college, it was
a joy of immense proportions to journey, in early June, exactly
five hundred and sixteen miles from our home in Grosse Pointe
Michigan to the Huron Mountain Club. Twenty thousand acres
in the upper peninsula of Michigan, on the southern shore of
Lake Superior, it was a virtual square six miles on a side with
twelve cold-water lakes, three trout streams, hundreds of miles
of walking trails. We were all privileged enough to go there
summer after summer. We knew that this was the nearest side
of an earthly paradise that came the day after harbor day,
would end as we left to go home and back to school, only to
return again in nine months time, year after year after year for
twenty years.

That particular morning I was up and out of bed early.
It was my habit in those days since I was nine. I was a trout
fisherman, introduced to the noble craft of anglers through my
mother and a long-time friend of hers, Onnie Aho. During the
academic years he taught manual training in a Detroit public
school. Every summer for nearly forty years he journeyed north
to work at the club, repairing members' furniture, making
more. But in his time off he took us fishing on one of the clubs
prehistoric glacial lakes. That was Onnie's real passion.

The armada he led in those days, it was during the
Second World War, were four in number including himself;
Mayo Schreiber, my cousin, John Wheat, another cousin, and
Reed Derby. We three admired Reed especially because at our

young ages of twelve or thirteen he had a special way with the gorgeous young waitress who came up from Marquette Michigan every summer to wait in the dining room at the club.

The club had a small fleet of Thompson rowboats on all twelve lakes, flat backed but very rowable. Not however like the elegant double ended and heavy plank-lapped vessels that Oscar had made. Oscar Knuusi was Finnish, as were many people in those days in Northern Michigan, he was the Club's boat builder for Fifty years. He was also the builder of many cabins at Huron Mountain.

We always carried a picnic lunch and dinner on those excursions. We couldn't waste precious fishing time building a fire for a hot meal. Onnie's wife Cecile made his, the Club's kitchen made up ours: peanut butter-jelly and lettuce-tomato, an orange and four graham crackers.

Onnie rowed us. We trolled, we were too young to cast a six ounce fly rod for the lurking small-mouth bass that hid among the ancient stumps along the thin bay of Rush Lake. But on virtually every trip with Onnie, between periodic pulls of his oars, would hook onto a nice bass, his Heddon rod arching under the weight of his catch. One very special catch was a 4 and 1/4 pound bass that, with enormous care and patience, he scared out of the ruins of a gigantic cedar tree that lay dried and dead way out into Rush Lake Bay.

I have not returned to that paradise for years now. I cannot wait to go back the summer after next. My wife will come with me. The memories of our childhood are with us forever. Elie Wiesel was right. Memory is the promise of the future.

Mr. Goddard was born in the Henry Ford Hospital in Detroit-Michigan on November 29, 1932 and can trace his Trout Fishing heritage to Hught Russel who arrived on our shores in 1745 in Chester County Pennsylvania. He in turn is the descendent of a long lineage of trout fisherfolk who claim their roots in Lockearnhead, Scotland. A town situated, as to be expected on Lock Earn, Near Glen Ogle and Saint Fillaus.

Honore Daumier
Les Plaisirs de la Peche
Cartoon
1842

Translation: *You are always in a hurry! Damn it we got here at noon and it is only 5:15...give me the time and I am sure that I will finally catch one!..*

A Fishing Talk Given at Yale

Ernest Schwiebert

"I don't know why I fish, or why others fish, except that it makes us think and feel."

—Roderick Haig-Brown, 1946

WHAT a wonderful party.

And what a wonderful purpose for a party, to say nothing of its magnificent setting: the Presidents' Rotunda at Yale. The portraits of Yale's historic leaders are a bit unsettling tonight. I am reminded, as I see them watching us in their academic robes and colorful hoods, of John Fitzgerald Kennedy's remark on the occasion of his celebration of Nobel Prize winners at the White House.

"I believe there has not been such an assemblage of intelligence in this room," the young president deadpanned, "since Thomas Jefferson dined alone."

The Presidents' Rotunda at Yale. It is a bit intimidating, and Allan Poole and I were a bit nervous, given our allegiance to Old Nassau, until we finally got to the bar. We were not entirely sure of ourselves. We decided to sit together, until we could decide on a strategy. We were clearly outnumbered in this coven of Old Bulldogs.

I intend to speak seriously of fishing tonight. What better place for serious fishing talk than Yale.

But before such serious matters, I believe that Alan and I are forced to agree that the *Yale Anglers' Journal* is a splendid idea, wonderfully executed and brought to life. We have long been aware of the unique fishing books in the jewel-box reliquary of the Beinecke Library, and the remarkable collection of David Wagstaff.

Princeton cannot quite match this astonishing plentitude of riches, although it has the collection of Carl Otto von Kienbusch, the books and manuscripts and papers of Eugene Virginius Connett, and the open-stack treasures of the Rockey Collection. And the parade of Princeton anglers and fishing authors is a bit unusual: William Cowper Prime, Henry Van Dyke, Grover Cleveland, Edward Ringwood Hewitt, Doctor Edgar Burke, Eugene Connett, Russell MacGregor , Otto von Kienbusch, Manning Barr, Philip Nash, Walter Steel, Victor Coty, Dana Storrs Lamb, and Austin Francis. It is only a partial list, but with all of its talent, these men never thought of anything like the *Yale Anglers' Journal*. And we salute you tonight.

It was a pleasure to see James Prosek again, and it was intriguing to learn of his new book project. But I must salute his *Compleat Angler*, not only for its subtle watercolors and and its contribution to Waltonia, but also for his manipulative skills in convincing Yale that a two-year travelling fellowship to fish was legitimate.

I have a grudging admiration for his success, since I once made a similar proposal to *National Geographic*, while a fellow member of the Anglers' Club of New York, Luis Marden, was its international editor .

Jonathan Trumbull Wright was a promising photographer with Geographic in those days, and we suggested a poetic picture essay, visiting the haunts and rivers that inspired the great British fishermen and their books. Wright was a skilled fisherman and alpinist himself, and I had known him since his boyhood in Aspen. We had worked together on magazine shoots before, including one in which Wright did his shooting with a helicopter harness under his armpits, and his boots planted on the skid. The starboard hatch had been removed, and he was shooting our MacKenzie boats as the helicopter hovered under the rim of the gorge, while we attempted to negotiate the wild chutes of the Black Canyon of the Gunnison.

We lost a boat in the first rapids below the Morrow Point boat access. No one was hurt, but the really dangerous stuff was overhead, as Wright worked outside the cockpit, with his boots braced on the skid.

And he became a great photographer.

Wright did the still photography for the American Bicentennial Expedition on Everest in 1976, reached its summit on a later television climb, and took cameras to the pinnacle of Ama Oablam in 1979. He was killed in Tibet a year later, in an avalanche on Minya Konka, which rises 24,790 feet above the Sichuan Province.[1] We would share no trip to Europe.

I can picture what we might have gotten there, on the rivers of England and Scotland, something like the little poem that James Prosek has achieved in The Compleat Angler, but with more characters. He has written a lovely book.

While still a graduate student in architecture and art history at Princeton, under Jean Labatut and Donald Drew Egbert, I spent considerable time filling out my dance card in undergraduate courses, and that moonlighting was spent at McCosh Hall. My mentors there included Alan Downer, who taught courses in theater; Carlos Heard Baker, the Hemingway biographer; and Gerald Eades Bentley, who was Murray Professor of English Literature. I knew Bentley and Baker quite well.

Their yardsticks were austere, and had they lived to witness the constructivist excesses of recent years, I am convinced that much subjective nonsense (like much post-modern architecture) would have been dismissed as doubtful conjecture. All disciplines are plagued with reiterations of the doubtful and the obvious. The story of Walton is straightforward and lovely, and the evocation of his landscapes and his rivers is a worthy purpose in itself.

I suspect The Compleat Angler was a lyric madrigal to fishing the gentle rivers of Middlesex and Derbyshire, and little more, other than its glimpses of a diverse and interesting life well-lived. Walton's fishing friends form a remarkable list, and a testimony to his education and wit, whatever their source. His little prose pastorale was not a clandestine allegory, a subversive document in a strife-torn England oppressed by Cromwell and his henchmen although Walton clearly supported Charles II.

Sometimes things are merely what they seem, and that remains enough. Sigmund Freud and Kenneth Starr notwithstanding, the cigar may only be a cigar. But our roots are wonderfully old.

We are here to celebrate an ancient and honorable sport, with roots reaching deep into antiquity. There are Egyptian sources as old as 2000 years before Christ, which depict rod fishing in the tomb murals of Beni Hasan. Chinese texts also describe rod fishing in those centuries. There are glazed tiles from the lost temple ruins of Nineveh, a thousand years later, depicting our sport in a flowing spring-fed pond. Such anglers may have caught trout, since there are such fish in the headwaters of the Tigris and Euphrates.

The Roman scholar and poet, Claudius Aelianus, tells of flyfishing and flymaking in the Second Century, in his *De Natura Animalium*.

Joseph Needham writes in his remarkable *History of Chinese Science*, which includes several shelves of scholarly and densely reasoned volumes, and more than a thousand pages of astonishing bibliographic material and notes, that brightly feathered lures were fashioned by Chinese artisans, four centuries before *De Natura Animalium*.

Needham includes an illustration from a scroll painting by the celebrated twelfth-century landscape painter, Ma Yuan, which clearly depicts a fishing reel, four centuries before its first appearance in English, in the little handbook published by Thomas Barker in 1651. There is no mistaking the device or its purpose, and Needham speculates that the reel may have logically evolved from Chinese gadgets used for preparing fibers and spinning cloth.

It would seem that Marco Polo might have brought more than spaghetti and silk and gunpowder in his baggage when he returned to Venice in 1295.

Our first mention of flyfishing in English, including descriptions of flymaking, is found in *The Boke of Saint Al-bans*, an artifact published by Wynken de Worde in 1496. There are contemporary writers who would like to discount the existence of its purported author, Dame Juliana Berners, the prioress of Sopwell nunnery at Saint Albans. Her *Treatyse of Fysshynge Wythe an Angle* was apparently written about 1420. There is an incomplete manuscript copy in the Wagstaff collection at Yale, the work of an unknown calligrapher of about 1450, when Berners was alive.

Despite the revisionists, I support the thesis of the late John MacDonald, the senior editor at *Fortune* who remains the finest American fishing historian. MacDonald was fascinated with Berners, and examined a number of copies of her *Treatyse* in the United Kingdom. He also explored the comments of the antiquarian, John Bale, who included the prioress in the literary biographies of his *Scriptorum Illustria Majoris Britanniae* of 1559.

Bale remains a bit controversial, since he was a Carmelite who turned against Rome, and campaigned bitterly for the principles of Martin Luther. He apparently participated in the theological quarrels of the sixteenth century, in which many British reformers were forced to leave the United Kingdom as Marian Exiles. Such exiles settled in English colonies at Geneva and Frankfurt-am-Main. But there is no evidence that Bale's strong religious convictions have prejudiced his observations on Berners, since they are laudatory and judicious. His *Scriptorum Illustria Majoris Britanniae* comments begin with a few expository facts:

> Juliana Barnes, illustris faemina, corporis et animis dotibus abundans, ac formae elegantia spect-abilis, inter alia humanae uitae folatia, venationes et aucupia in magnis habebat delicis.[2]

MacDonald farther tells us that Bale used a colleague as his principal firsthand source, and the biographical treatise *De Viris Illustribus, Sive de Scriptoribus Britannicus*. It was the work of John Leland, who had served as court librarian and antiquarian to Henry VIII, and had died in 1552. But MacDonald did not stop there.

William Burton was another British antiquarian who was familiar with Leland and Bale, and was actually in possession of Leland's notes and papers. Burton presented these notes and papers to the Bodeleian Library at Oxford in 1632. Burton lived within a century of Leland, and spent decades pouring over the collated books and manuscripts that Leland had discovered in his investigations, which had included most of the castles, manorhouses, monasteries, convents, universities, and private libraries throughout the British realm, at the orders and authorization of Henry VIII.

Among the books and manuscripts in the possession of the Bishop of Ely, Doctor John Moore, was included a complete copy of *The Boke of Saint Albans*. His gracefully embellished church suffered great damage at the hands of Cromwellian troops, and the angling fraternity is fortunate that this book was not lost when most of its religious sculpture and icons were wantonly smashed.

There are handwritten annotations in this copy of Berners, which is still found at Cambridge University, a few miles south of Ely. MacDonald explored the book in great detail, and his paleographic studies confirm that they are in the hand of William Burton.

The opening handwritten notes are based upon Burton's thorough knowledge of Leland's entire library, as well as his notes and papers, with the help of Burton's own scholarly perceptions of the fifteenth century:

> This book was made by the Lady Julian Berners, daughter of Sir James Berners of Berners Roding in Essex; Knight; and sister to Richard Lord Berners. She was the Lady Prioresse of Sopewelle, a nunnery neare Saint Albans; in which Abbey of Saint Albans, this was first printed in 1486. She was still living in 1460, according to John Bale.

The disciplines of history do not rest merely on the printed word. Both oral histories and contemporaneous accounts have often proved correct, and I believe we should trust witnesses who lived in or near the period in contention, unless they had some obvious axe to grind. It is usually quite easy to identify the furtive undertones of malice. John Leland was highly regarded in his time, and in the century that followed. His access to the finest libraries of the United Kingdom was unique, and Leland died only sixty-odd years after the publication of *The Boke of Saint Albans*. And I rest my case.

We must remain skeptical and wary of revisionism, as well as its ulterior purposes, since dissenting opinions make waves, and attract more attention, than scholarly affirmations of our heritage. Few readers seem to see the temptations implicit in willful dissent, since it draws the historian himself into the limelight. Thomas Steams Eliot understood these sins in *Murder in the Cathedral*:

> The last temptation is the greatest treason; To do the right deed, for the wrong reason.

I was among the few who were privileged to know the British expatriate, Roderick Haig-Brown, and I treasure our encounters in New York, Sun Valley , Jackson Hole, and Aspen. I first met him through Ed Zern, at a dinner party in Scarsdale, which lasted long after midnight. The photographer Dan Callaghan and I once drove from Portland to Campbell River, and we spent a four-day weekend with the writer, in the book-filled atelier where he worked. It was late winter and there were migrating grosbeaks in the orchard, which lay just beyond his writing desk. Fitful February sun danced on the dark river. We recorded our conversations and Callaghan took pictures, and we got to see the poet in his British Columbia landscapes. Haig-Brown cherished our sport, with its alchemy of history, tradition, literature, athletic grace, science, and art. Such convictions are obvious in the beautiful closing paragraph of *A River Never Sleeps*.

He confesses that he does not fully understand why he chooses to fish, or why others fish, except that it makes us think and feel. I cannot think of two better reasons for anything. Haig-Brown later tells us that everything involved in our sport is beautiful, like the rivers themselves, and everything they nurture. He concludes that were it not for the swift poetry of rivers, with their pewtery light in the rain, the trembling pull of their currents, and the feel of their cobble under his feet, he would fish less often.

And he closes *A River Never Sleeps* with the observation that he fishes simply to be near rivers, and concludes that if that sweet epiphany is true, he is grateful that he finally thought of it. All lives have epiphanies of sorts, sudden insights both large and small, and the trick is simply not to miss their meanings. I think that I fish for beauty.

My first epiphany came more than sixty years ago, on an unpaved country road in southern Michigan. I saw a man fishing, and asked my mother to stop. The little river was crystalline and smooth, with a pea-gravel bottom, and its currents slipped past cedar roots and sweepers. The flow was relatively swift, and tumbled past his legs. His golden line was working back and forth in the sun, in a noiseless ballet of lazy rhythms, before dropping his flies tight against the fallen logs. There was a splash and he tightened. It was not a large fish.

But it fought splashily against his dancing rod before it finally came to net. I scrambled down from the bridge, and the man held it in the net until I reached him. My fishing had been limited to bullheads in muddy creeks, and pumpkinseeds and perch off our Michigan dock, but this fish was a revelation, and in the words of my favorite New Zealand fisherman, the colorful Hughie MacDowell, it seemed like a fish straight from God's own mold.

It was a brook trout of six inches. But its flanks were like a jeweler's tray of opals and moonstones and rubies, its bright tangerine fins edged in ebony and alabaster, and its olive back and shoulders like the vermiculated endpapers of a rare French edition. It was an epiphany, a bright potshard of living poetry, and I have never been happy with anything else. It was beautiful.

Such beauty is increasingly important, perhaps our only antidote to the brash cacophonies that plague these demotic times. Trout fishing is quite beautiful. Its skills offer an equilibrium between history, tradition, physical dexterity and grace, strength, logic, problem solving, esthetics, science, our powers of observation and diagnosis, perceptions, and the full spectrum of our experience. Our tackle and fly boxes are quite beautiful too, and the serial chess games of tactics and entomology and flymaking remain unique.

Beauty. The sport is filled with beauty. We share the passion for bright rivers tumbling toward the salt, the deft choreography of swifts and swallows working to a hatch of fly, and the quicksilver poetry of the fish themselves. And in seeking such beauty, in the crystalline magic of trout water, we may discover that beauty is the most endangered thing of all.

[1]The alpinist Rick Ridgeway led the Minya Konka expedition, which included Yvon Chouinard. Ridgeway and I delivered eulogies for Wright, at the Aspen Institute for Humanistic Studies. Ridgeway recounts his death in *Below Another Sky* which was recently published by Henry Holt.

[2] There are a number of translations of these words, each seeming to reflect the prejudices of the author in question. Neither Joseph Haslewood in 1810, nor William Blades in 1881, could quite bring himself to admit that a beautiful woman could possess both a thorough knowledge of the field sports, and also be prioress of a nunnery. But as MacDonald points out, the knowledge of sport obtained from her beginings as a noblewoman of Bemers Roding was quite plausible, and such expertise would not be lost after her subsequent vows as a nun. I believe the best translation of Bale's description of Bemers might be the following:

> Julian Barnes, illustrious woman, eminently abounding in gifts of body and spirit, and remarkable for her physical form and elegance; among the solaces of human life she venerated the field sports in the highest estimation.

Infamous Princeton alumni, trout fisherman, and author of numerous titles including Death of A River Keeper, Trout *(Two Volumes), and the* Compleat Schwiebert, *Ernest Schwiebert was hoodwinked with promises of an open bar and young women into speaking at the first annual Yale Anglers' Journal fundraising dinner.*

Carl Armin Hansen
Fishermen
Ink on Paper
1920

Noli Me Tangere

Tyler Welti

Scales rise. A mind reels, design stripped by tugs on the tip;
The taut line like a tree-house radio
Talks in converse tremors, an austere lingo.
Hook and eye lure us toward our summit.
Whoso learn to cast, to seek and find
Foreign promise, to tie the perfect knot
And fly into the dogfight: I have sought
The rainbow's violent visceral end of the line.
At dinner time, dine with your divined trophy,
But as for me, alas, it allures no more:
Fish grime beneath my fingernails, in the sore
Hook-torn thumb, was our matrimony.
It shivers in mind, as shadow in the creek,
And wild still to ponder, not to keep.

Tyler Welti is a senior at Yale University, a native Californian, and an avid fisherman. He grew up fishing Santa Ynez River, Lake Cachuma, and the local estuaries in the Santa Barbara area. Fishing led to an interested in nature writing, especially poetry, environmental education, and understanding ecosystem values. He regards the wild trout as a perfection of form and beauty, and feels that with such perfection of nature, catch and release is the only way to fish. A surfer at heart, Tyler misses the waves of the Pacific and can often be found riding the black asphalt streets of New Haven on his long board skateboard.

Chinese Communist Party Poster
People and Fish Jumping For Joy
From *Chinese Propoganda Posters*
1978

Editor's Note: Printed just after the end of the cultural revolution, this poster portrays the contributions of women to society. These beautiful girls, along with their bountiful catch of fish, are a symbol of wealth in China display the country's health and prosperity.

Aldo Leopold in the Global Age:
Toward a Contemporary Environmental Ethic
Daniel Smith

T HE sun is well up from the horizon and radiant, embedded in a deep blue sky. Two feet of snowpack glisten beneath our grove of white birches, crisp and quiet in the still air. The temperature is just now creeping above zero. My morning chore is splitting wood, which today is no chore at all because the cold is deep enough so that stout logs yield to a mere tap of the ax. The dryness of this Canadian air and the sun's warmth keep me surprisingly comfortable in just a wool shirt. It is good to be out and good to feel independent, making use of the trees that grow with such vigor in our cool, moist New England woods.

When I burn the remains of this tree it will produce heat and smoke, releasing carbon and other elements into the atmosphere. But I know that other trees will grow in its place next summer, absorbing carbon from the air and nutrients from the soil to make leaves, sap, and wood fiber, folding a succession of individuals into the continuity and stability of this woodland community. Whether I am a member of it or an invader is arguable; I fancy myself the former. But here at my wood pile the cycles of my life mesh at least in part with the seasonal and elemental cycles of the woods. I find this mixture of physical health and mental order very satisfying. It feels good and it makes sense.

It is tempting to suggest that my experience is simply "natural" and, therefore, "good"—that there is some sort of absolute standard at work here. But history insists that this is not so, that notions of what is right and good result largely from changing circumstances and the ongoing evolution of human culture. Although some values are nearly universal across different cultures and endure for thousands of years—such as holding that murder is morally wrong—many of the values of a given culture will evolve through time, sometimes quickly, sometimes very slowly. New stages in this evolution often become distilled and clarified by individuals who perceive change before or more clearly than their peers and reach society with a compelling vision that matches the experience and aspirations of others, that somehow feels right. In the realm of environmental ethics Aldo Leopold was such a person. Although he died in 1948, Leopold has become, through his writing, a mentor for many land managers and conservationists today.

Near the end of his life, after practicing and teaching forestry and wildlife management for four decades, Leopold set down his thoughts on how people do and should relate to "the land." He saw the land not just as a physical unit, but as a community of life, a complex and interdependent group of organisms.[1] Leopold's moral proposal, which he called "a land ethic," outlined the need to expand the ethical community beyond human beings "to include soils, water, plants, animals, or collectively: the land."

> In short, a land ethic changes the role of *Homo sapiens* from conqueror of the land-community to plain member and citizen of it. It implies respect for his fellow-members, and also respect for the community as such ... A thing is right when it tends to preserve the integrity, stability and beauty of the biotic community. It is wrong when it tends otherwise.[2]

This passage is from the final section of Leopold's book *A Sand County Almanac*. It is preceded by a series of musings on natural history, ecology, and conservation which form an eloquent foundation for his ethical proposal. Leopold's writing is not marked by a scholarly tone or by complex and erudite abstractions. Rather, his prose exhibit the detail, perspective, and grace of someone who has not only studied and learned, but who has experienced the things that interest him. Recounting some of his forest adventures, Leopold comments that "Every farm woodland, in addition to yielding lumber, fuel, and posts, should provide its owner a liberal education. This crop of wisdom never fails, but it is not always harvested. I here record some of the many lessons I have learned in my own woods."[3]

Leopold's land ethic carries special meaning for land managers because his philosophy reflects a balance of practicality and morality. In suggesting that actions that do not tend to "preserve the integrity, stability and beauty of the biotic community" are wrong—not unfortunate or impractical, but wrong—he staked out a clear moral position that was unprecedented in his day and remains radical in the eyes of many people. Yet he stressed that such an ethic is grounded in biological and ecological reality. Leopold described the flow of energy through trophic pyramids as one of the most fundamental characteristics of ecosystem function and noted that changes in the flow of energy occur as a natural, evolutionary process. But he added, "Evolutionary changes ... are usually slow and local. Man's invention of tools has enabled him to make changes of unprecedented violence, rapidity and scope."[4] Working with nature rather then against her, he argued, is both an ethical imperative and in keeping with basic ecological and evolutionary principles.

Leopold hoped the land ethic would help society navigate the increasingly complex and difficult relationship between people and nature in the 20th century. "An ethic may be regarded as a mode of guidance for meeting ecological situations so new or intricate, or involving such deferred reactions, that the path of social expediency is not discernible to the average individual." Recognizing that the expansion of the ethical community is an historical process capable of responding to both social and ecological needs, Leopold urged the development of a land ethic as "an evolutionary possibility and an ecological necessity."[5] He believed that to maintain the health of the land that supports us, we must change our way of thinking, not just our technology and our laws.

As I work in the woods, I find comfort and inspiration in these words written nearly a half-century ago. Within my limited sphere of influence—at my wood pile in winter, fishing in the spring, in my garden in summer, and hunting in the fall—I have embraced Leopold's land ethic. This is partly because of my own life-affirming experience with the land and partly because I fit into a tradition, with teachers I can draw upon. Many of my friends and colleagues share these values, as do millions of other people across the country. The basic premise of respect for life in all its forms is surely a cornerstone of the environmental movement. And who is not some sort of environmentalist these days? Membership in environmental organizations has soared since the 1970s and polls show the environment to be a major issue of enduring concern. I have company in my beliefs, and there is solace in that.

But when I come inside to read the paper or any of the environmental journals I try to keep up with, my sense of harmony dissolves. Indeed, much is wrong with the world, and the specter of a disintegrating environment often haunts my thoughts of the future. We seem destined to lose between one-quarter and one-half the species on Earth in the next fifty years —which is to say, in my lifetime.[6,7] The chlorofluorocarbons we have released into the atmosphere are eating away at the stratospheric ozone layer. This is not a theory but a fact, and it is likely to cause 200,000 additional skin-cancer deaths in the United States during that same half-century.[8] Nobody knows what it will do to other creatures with whom we share the earth. By burning fossil fuels, we are altering the carbon cycle to such an extent that the earth may warm by 1.5°C to 4.5°C in the next century.[9] Such a warming is likely to inundate coastal areas destabilize agriculture, and degrade forests and other terrestrial ecosystems. That, of course, brings us back full circle to the extinction of species, which tends to accelerate as the health of ecosystems declines. Underlying all of these problems is the continuing growth of the Earth's human population, which now stands at more than 5.5 billion and may approach 11 billion by the year 2030.[10] Looking beyond my woodpile to the Earth and its communities, things simply look bleak.

Why, then, at a time when the environmental movement is flourishing, are we not having more success? Is it that we still have not made enough converts, either at home or abroad? Have we not done enough to educate our children? Not enough to organize the grass roots, to lobby government and reform industry? Are there too many complacent people? Too many greedy people who just don't care? Too many people with too little money or too little food to be able to look beyond immediate survival?

To all these questions the environmentalist chorus answers a hearty "yes," and that affirmation sums up its dominant outlook today. We say we need more. More education, more activism, more reform and regulation, more money to fight for the cause.

Yet this view leaves something missing. It does not ask us to look at ourselves, to consider carefully, as Leopold did, the material results and the ethical implications of our own behavior, of the choices we make every day. For it is, after all, the behavior of individuals and groups, multiplied millions of times over, that has lead to our current predicament and which may, eventually, get us out of it. To be most useful, our self-examination must have as its beginning the development of a true ecological understanding of our place in the world, an understanding of how our actions affect all the members of the biological community, both locally and globally, both tomorrow and into the next century.

What the new and seemingly intractable environmental problems suggest about the human role in world affairs is that while the sheer magnitude of human activity has surely increased—there are more people doing more things on more acres of land than ever before—the very nature of that activity has changed as well. Today the issues are fundamentally different. Many of the changes now being wrought are so subtle or indirect in the short-term that they are not readily visible and can only be perceived in the abstract or with sustained empirical measurement. Yet, paradoxically, they may be truly devastating in the long run. Ozone depletion, global warming, and the world-wide loss of biological diversity typify this category. Clearcutting, erosion, waste disposal, and the loss of natural areas—problems that can be readily seen or felt—belong in a more traditional, local class of issues. Of course, there is also a merging of these local and global scales, of the tangible and intangible, as local problems multiplied enough times yield global results. Hence the biodiversity crisis, which stems from millions of individual actions on millions of different parcels of land in thousands of different ecosystems. In addition, the increasingly global economy systematically hides the environmental cost of many products. Supermarket beef may come from clearcut rain forest or from overgrazed Nevada desert, but that is invisible to consumers. The current collection of cause and effect linkages between people and the environment is thus vastly different from that which existed fifty or even twenty-five years ago. Developing an understanding of one's place in the world requires that these differences be recognized.

Columbus Day weekend, 1991. I am driving north on I-93, leaving behind the pressure of work, pressure that has been building relentlessly for several months. Hours and miles ahead are relaxed days with friends on a lake in the Maine woods. I will fish, walk, read, and paddle. I hope to become myself again, or at least make a start in the right direction. As I cross into southern New Hampshire the traffic remains remarkably heavy even as the suburbs of Boston fall behind. My speed is a steady thirty miles per hour. I look ahead at hundreds of cars, and a glance to my rear shows an equally-packed mirror image. We are all moving relentlessly north away from the urban core, seeking a few days of respite. The monotony and consistency of the traffic stream is striking. As my eyes fix on one car after another, I cannot stop wondering what the thousands of cars on this road—and the millions like them on similar roads leaving cities across the country—add up to. How much energy do we all use? How much pollution spews from our engines? How much oil was drilled, refined and moved around the globe to make us go?

While I cannot answer precisely, I know that these

questions lead to deeply troubling answers. When compared to the energy used by other animals or by people until the most recent and tiny fraction of human history—or, for that matter, the majority of people alive today—the energy I will use in these several hours of travel is enormous. The impacts of burning these ten or so gallons of gas stretch far afield: from drilling, extraction and refining, perhaps in environmentally fragile areas; to the energy used shipping it across the country or around the world; to the compounds emanating from my exhaust pipe, including sulfur and nitrogen which will degrade local and regional air quality and eventually return to earth as acid rain, and carbon dioxide, which will hasten global warming. Considering these things, I feel ill at ease, guilty, and I consider turning back. But after stopping for lunch and collecting my thoughts I continue on my way, knowing that friends are waiting for me and that I need this break badly. But I continue to wonder about the tradeoffs. When are the costs of such extravagance justified?

What does Leopold's land ethic have to say about my experience or about the new class of environmental ills? Not much, on the surface of it. He was a land manager concerned with the impacts of that management on nature. He might have something to say about roads displacing wildlife habitat, but many of the problems that concern me were unknown in his day. There was little suspicion that burning fossil fuels, for instance, would give rise to the problems we now face. Leopold wrote about the ethics of how we treat the land through activities like farming, forestry, and recreation, not the indirect effects of actions as seemingly disconnected to nature as driving a car. But a closer look at Leopold's underlying premise—that ethics must evolve as a means of guiding human behavior, especially in situations where the implications of that behavior are not obvious or fully understood—shows that it has a great deal to say. Leopold could not have foreseen the particular course human impacts would take or the mechanisms through which they would occur. By emphasizing the need to draw a more inclusive circle around the ethical community, however, he implicitly recognized the need for a continuing evolution of ethics, an evolution that keeps pace with changes in human behavior and its ever-widening sphere of influence. While the land ethic at first seems out of date or at least incomplete in the face of our current predicament, Leopold's reasoning behind it gives a firm base on which to build even in times of great change. Rather than limiting us to the views of an earlier time, his land ethic can urge us on to a new understanding of what he sought fifty years ago—an understanding of what we are doing in the world and how our ideas of right and wrong need to adapt to guide our actions.

Leopold's plea to enlarge the ethical community has been taken up wholeheartedly by the environmental movement and, if the endangered species act is any indication, has been at least partially accepted by American society at large. However, his underlying assertion that we need to periodically readjust our view of how we fit into that community has gone largely unnoticed.

While policy analysts and environmental specialists debate institutional and technical solutions to the new global class of environmental problems, these issues are rarely considered within an ethical framework. We are highly selective in looking at these issues, as well as more traditional ones, on a personal level and with questions of right and wrong in mind. Few of us invoke overarching principles, but rather single-out those issues that have the greatest personal appeal and require the least sacrifice. This selectivity is further reinforced by political and environmental leaders, always fearful of offending voters or potential donors.

Cutting old-growth forests is assumed to be wrong. But is it right to drive or fly a thousand miles for vacation or to live fifty miles from one's place of work? It is seen as wrong to use disposable goods without recycling. But is it right to have large families in a crowded world knowing that each member will use many times the resources and energy consumed by a person in a developing country? It seen as wrong to hunt whales or wide-eyed baby seals. But is it right to live in low-density suburban or rural housing that displaces wildlife habitat? These actions all have profound effects on the environment and on our fellow creatures, yet they are rarely scrutinized and they do not appear on many conservation hit lists. We have embraced Leopold's land ethic as it applied to the 1940s while hardly noticing the changes of recent decades. We have succumbed to an inertia of ethical reasoning as if our feet were stuck in mud.

Most of us tend to adopt moral views on those issues that appear obvious and clear-cut. We tend to shy away from moral pronouncements on issues that are inconvenient or psychologically troublesome. It is not easy to exercise the discipline of driving fewer miles when the effects of automobiles cannot be seen first hand, when housing near urban centers is unaffordable, or when cities offer few well-designed open spaces for recreation. It is not easy for people who love children to ponder the future impacts of their unborn children. It is not easy to resist distant vacations, especially when they are dressed in the rosy garb of "ecotourism."

Focusing on these issues creates considerable tension because it strikes at the core of our values and lifestyle. It raises the specter of being judged on our most private beliefs or regulated in our most cherished activities. This problem is exacerbated by the long time-frame of many environmental issues compared to other ethical problems. Society must make decisions on the death penalty and prison sentences because criminals are here today. Women and couples grapple with the question of abortion because pregnancies are occurring now. Environmental degradation, on the other hand, is often an incremental process taking decades or more, so we feel less of a sense of urgency. Only if we look clearly and unflinchingly at a more distant future, especially at our childrens' future, does the urgency return.

A dialogue about these lifestyle issues can help people make personal choices, for very few of the issues surrounding environmental behavior are clear-cut. They are, in fact, highly complex and, in the absence of focused attention, just as likely to spawn ambivalence as firm decisions and changed behavior. It sounds noble to advocate abandoning the automobile, but how will we get to work? It would be best environmentally to limit families to one child, but who is to judge what this would cost in human terms? Virtually all of the materials we use—wood, metal, plastic—come with an unseen environmental price tag, yet they help people lead productive and fulfilling lives.

These tradeoffs leave us in the short run with a balancing act that has environmental costs on one side and human benefits on the other. Our task is to strike that balance in a way that will ensure the long-term health and sustainability of both nature and people. Where popular sentiment is strong, the tradeoffs can be politically determined and implemented through regulation or financial incentives. Where political solutions lag behind, however, or where choices are too complex or subtle for legal generalizations, individual responsibility must carry us. With questions of personal choice—where to live, how to travel, how to spend money—ethics can serve, as Leopold suggested, "as a mode of guidance."

By combining a basic respect for life—a land ethic—with a clear understanding and honest assessment of the repercussions of our actions we can begin to move in the direction of balance. It is not enough to care deeply. It is not enough to understand how things work. Both are necessary. Moreover, caring and understanding will be of little use if they do not lead to concrete action. Just as Leopold stressed that a land ethic must be tied both to moral principles and to ecological reality, so too must an evolving environmental ethic be tied to a sense of pragmatic action.

Ethical dilemmas aside, we shy away from the implications of our own behavior because we are caught in such a strong cultural and material tide. We are locked into a system that is solidly based on the massive and extravagant use of resources, and there is no easy way out. Our cities have been designed to foster long commutes rather than discourage them. Our mass transit is inadequate. The products we buy are manufactured inefficiently, and global trade, the good mantra of this decade, encourages shipment from far away places regardless of the true impacts of foreign manufacturing and long-distance transport. Politicians insist that continuous economic growth (and, many economists would argue, population growth) is necessary despite the fact that we possess finite resources. And that growth is measured by summing up all economic activity, regardless of its true value. Thus, the jobs created in cleaning up an oil spill are weighed as a net good, while eroded soil washes to the sea unnoticed. All the while popular culture insist that acquisition of more bright and shiny products is always desirable.

In the absence of an infrastructure, an economic system, and a culture that fosters environmentally sound behavior, the challenge of leading a truly "good life"—whatever that turns out to be—is nearly overwhelming. Only by linking together a new ethic, greater understanding, and reform of organizations and infrastructure can we begin to move in the direction of long-term balance. Historically, such massive social changes have occurred slowly and without intent or planning. It is a measure of the current situation's urgency that these changes need to be guided purposefully and brought about rapidly. Whether we are successful or not will depend, ultimately, on our ability to transform the human heart and mind, among the few natural resources not now in short supply.

I have finished cutting wood for today, I have had lunch and a rest by the fire, and it is time to go for a ski in all this fresh snow. I drive to the end of our road and meet a friend at the beginning of the East Pasture Loop. I thought of driving north to the Kilkenny but decided on something closer to home. I am a little disappointed at not seeing new country, but soon I am happy with the familiar scenery and the chance to pay more attention to the subtleties of our local woods. William Least Heat Moon has written that "no place, in theory, is boring of itself. Boredom lies only with the traveler's limited perception and his failure to explore deeply enough."[11] I find this to be true of repetition as well as places that seem dull the first time around. I am comfortable in familiar surroundings and see things on this trip I have not before. The deep green of spruce tops against an even deeper blue sky is as beautiful to me as any mountain valley the Rockies have to offer.

My impact is still too great. I suspect my net presence remains, environmentally, a negative. Living in the country, where work, stores and friends are far apart, I drive more than twice as many miles each year as I did living in Boston. My office is heated with oil. I buy food that comes from industrial farms in California, and other goods from around the world. I have a long way to go, and my slow progress frustrates me. But between my wood pile and my exploring close to home, I am making a start. I find, through the satisfaction these things bring, that it is not so painful after all.

1. Leopold, Aldo. A Sand County Almanac. New York: Oxford University Press, 1949.
2. Ibid.
3. Ibid.
4. Ibid.
5. Ibid.
6. Ehrlich, P.R. and E.O. Wilson. "Biodiversity Studies: Science and Policy." Science, 1991. p. 253.
7. Wilson, E.O. The Diversity of Life. Cambridge: Belknap Press of Harvard University, 1992.
8. Brown, L.R., ed. State of the World 1993. New York: W.W. Norton, 1993.
9. Brown, L.R., H. Kane, and E. Ayres. Vital Signs 1993. New York: W.W. Norton, 1993.
10. Ibid.
11. Least Heat Moon, W. Blue Highways. Boston: Little Brown and Co., 1982.

** This essay was originally published in the June 1995 issue of Appalachia.
© Appalachian Mountain Club.

Daniel Smith is a doctoral candidate at Yale's School of Forestry and Environmental Studies. He has worked previously in the fields of ecosystem ecology (at the University of Pennsylvania), environmental planning (at the National Park Service), and environmental education (at the Appalachian Mountain Club). His research focuses on the historical and social context of forest policy and conservation in northern New England. He is especially interested in understanding the embedded and often unquestioned cultural assumptions, social structures, and power relationships that inhibit our ability to respond to the rapidly changing nature of environmental problems.

Bob White
Fly Tyer
Ink Drawing
2001

Bob White has been a full-time professional painter and illustrator since 1980. His work is influenced by the scenes of sporting life in Alaska, Argentina, and near his home in rural Minnesota where he lives with his wife Lisa. He works in a variety of mediums and some more of his pieces are visible on the internet at www.whitefishstudio.com.

How To Catch Fish with Flies
Ed Zern

Some wiseguy once defined a fishing line as a piece of string with a worm on one end and a damn fool on the other.

This is a silly definition, of course—for many fishermen use flies instead of worms. They think it is more hoity-toity. If worms cost two bits apiece, and you could dig Royal Coachmen and Parmacheene Belles out of the manure pile, they would think differently. This is called human nature.

Fly fishermen spend hours tying little clumps of fur and feathers on hooks, trying to make a trout fly that looks like a real fly. But nobody has ever seen a natural insect trying to mate with a Fanwig Ginger Quill.

Of course, every once in a while a fly flyfisherman catches a trout on a trout fly, and he thinks this proves something. It doesn't. Trout eat mayflies, burnt matches, small pieces of inner tube, each other, caddis worms, Dewey buttons, crickets, lima beans, Colorado spinners, and almost anything else they can get in their fool mouths. It is probable they think the trout fly is some feathers tied to a hook. Hell, they're not blind. They just want to see how it tastes.

Trout flies are either wet flies or dry flies, depending on whether they are supposed to sink or float. If you ask a wet-fly fisherman why a natural insect would be swimming around like crazy under water, he gets huffy and walks away.

Many fishermen think trout are color-blind, but that is nothing to what trout think of fishermen.

The late Ed Zern was one of the great outdoor humorists of the twentieth century. His regular column in Field and Stream *and numerous books assured readers that they were not the only ones not catching fish, and any success that they were having was certainly not due to their skill.*